Integrated Management Systems

Leading Strategies and Solutions

Wayne Pardy and Terri Andrews

GOVERNMENT INSTITUTES
An imprint of
The Scarecrow Press, inc.
Lanham • Toronto • Plymouth, UK
2010

 **Government Institutes**

Published by Government Institutes
An imprint of The Scarecrow Press, Inc.
A wholly owned subsidary of The Rowman & Littlefield Publishing Group, Inc.
4501 Forbes Boulevard, Suite 200, Lanham, Maryland 20706
http://www.govinstpress.com

Estover Road, Plymouth PL6 7PY, United Kingdom

British Library Cataloguing in Publication Information Available

Library of Congress Cataloging-in-Publication Data

Pardy, Wayne G.
  Integrated management systems : leading strategies and solutions / Wayne Pardy and Terri Andrews.
     p. cm.
  Includes bibliographical references and index.
  ISBN 978-0-86587-196-0 (cloth : alk. paper) — ISBN 978-1-60590-658-4 (electronic)
  1. Management. 2. Management information systems. I. Andrews, Terri, 1957– II. Title.
  HD31.P288 2010
  658.4'038011—dc22   2009026062

∞™ The paper used in this publication meets the minimum requirements of American National Standard for Information Sciences—Permanence of Paper for Printed Library Materials, ANSI/NISO Z39.48-1992.

Printed in the United States of America

This book is dedicated to our two-legged children, Beth and Mark; our four-legged children, Colby, Louie, Eddie, and Koko; and our angel children, Cody and Sophie.

It's also dedicated to our moms, Nora and Jean. And to our fathers, Chrissy and Garland, who we know would be very proud if they were here.

CONTENTS

CONTENTS

CONTENTS

INTRODUCTION

The purpose of an integrated management system is to help provide a clear representation of all the features of your respective management system pieces, to show how they impact and complement one other, and to demonstrate how their relationship assists in managing the respective management systems risks of the organization.

Of course, one of the principle objectives is to help ensure synergy and to provide for less duplication and more rationalization of common approaches, ideas, and tools.

The global realities of today's business environment are forcing many individuals and organizations to change and adapt, and quickly. There is no longer the luxury of studying, hedging, and waiting until things "return to normal." Normal will be determined by those who have the foresight and vision to take control of the present to help shape a brighter future. That brighter future can be impacted by the maturity and effectiveness of the management systems that help guide a business through its core organizational objectives while staying financially competitive and in business.

The aim of an integrated management system is toward those organizations that have instituted a single management system that has as its focus two or more management system approaches. Whether or not those management systems are commercially available, based on international standards, or developed and designed in-house, the effort to rationalize an integrated approach to these management systems is often a reasonable one, yet one with some initial challenges about how best to approach the effort.

The objective of this book is to profile many of the important issues and challenges associated with this integrated management system journey and to highlight many of the practical considerations for the effective development and implementation of your integrated management system approach. Whether or not you decide on certifying or registering your integrated management system is up to you. This book is intended to profile the things you'll need to consider and demonstrate should you wish to travel down the road of having one management system that encompasses all of your other management systems pieces into one system.

Whether you have an existing formal system or not, it is always wise to adopt a structured business process approach to your management system development. The task is not for the faint of heart. Aside from the normal business and financial challenges, there will be other barriers in the form of personality- and people-based resistance that you will have to manage. But the strength of your business case should hinge on the fact that the benefits of one comprehensive, rationalized, and coherent system can serve the divergent business needs while giving you maximum flexibility.

This book can be used as a road map to assist in identifying standards, tasks, recommended approaches, and processes. Our approach begins by looking at your business environment as a whole while seeking to find the balance of establishing and achieving its objectives and core processes. It offers both practical items for consideration and key ideas and principles worthy of discussion and debate within your own organization in order for you and your management team to make intelligent, informed decisions about the future and focus of your integrated management systems. It puts you "in the driver's seat" and profiles the real-world issues each and every individual charged with designing and implementing management systems face on a day-to-day basis.

The bottom line of integrated management systems: a guideline for a more efficient, effective, and productive business that has rationalized the logic of its business practices, markets, and risk with the goal of a healthier balance sheet.

A PRIMER ON INTEGRATED MANAGEMENT SYSTEMS

Many times the best place to start is at the beginning. So it is with this book on integrated management systems. Perhaps it would be beneficial to start with a definition of an integrated management system, right from the start, to set the foundation for the ideas contained in this book. So first of all, what is a management system? Simply stated, a management system is the framework of policies, systems, processes, and procedures used (hopefully effectively) to ensure that an organization can fulfill all tasks required to achieve its defined business objectives.

It may be argued that some organizations function quite well without a formalized or structured management system. Competition in their respective area of business may be limited, risk may be minimal, or perceived as minimal, and activities may be uncomplicated or mature. Processes and business knowledge reside in the heads of the individuals who manage and work for the company, and while those people are around, the company thrives. However, if circumstances change, a company's strengths can become its weaknesses. When customer bases increase, competition is introduced or increases, more complicated processes are introduced, regulators impose new or more stringent requirements, or skilled and knowledgeable personnel move on, the organization becomes at risk and the need for a more formalized management process emerges.

Larger organizations or those with complicated activities are more likely to have clearly defined processes, documented procedures, well-developed personnel hierarchies, and more sophisticated record keeping. The need for structure to manage risk and to ensure consistency, efficiency, and continuing capability is easy to understand. It is more obvious that systems are required to provide order and maintain effectiveness.

To ensure effective control and to meet the requirements of customers and stakeholders, including regulatory bodies and the community at large, more and more organizations are implementing formal and strategic management systems. Depending on what is needed to maintain control and guide improvement, different system models may be used. Some of the more recognized management system models include:

- ISO 9001   (Quality Management Systems)

- ISO 14001   (Environmental Management Systems)

- OHSAS 18001   (Occupational Health and Safety Management Systems)

- CSA Z1000   (OHS Management System / Canada)

- ANSI/AIHA Z10-2005   (OHS Management System / United States)

- ILO-OSH 2001   (OHS Management System / International)

Depending upon the type and complexity of organizational activities, the decision may be made to implement more than one system. For example, it is not uncommon for organizations to create separate management systems to control quality, occupational health and safety, or environmental areas and sometimes, discreet functions within those areas.

But the success of even the best systems can be undermined if those systems do not consider or complement each other. It's been suggested that without a holistic approach to their management and interaction, even good systems can result in bureaucracy, duplication, and suboptimization. In other words, they can become dysfunctional.

Over the past couple of decades, companies large and small have been driven by customer, regulatory, industry, and internal motivators to implement quality, health and safety, and environmental (QHSE) management systems. While these can operate separately, all typically share a set of common characteristics and there is undeniable value in managing them in an integrated fashion, provided that there is compatibility. That value comes from resource optimization and work execution rationalization. In other words, the old cliché of working "smarter and not harder" is given credence. Compatibility also becomes an important consideration.

ISO Guide 72, the guideline that provides those who are tasked with writing standards with a framework of common management system requirements, defines *compatibility* as the "suitability of similar standards for use together under specific conditions to fulfill relevant requirements without causing unacceptable interactions."[1] In other words, if common characteristics can be rationalized and implemented in a shared fashion, without duplication or conflict, the management systems are deemed to be compatible.

The common characteristics of some of the well-known management system models include:

- Policies, and the objectives and targets associated with them

- Planning that reflects the strategic and management system objectives and uses factual information flowing from the management system

- Organizational structure defining roles, responsibilities, and authorities for personnel performing work that can impact upon the management system objectives

- Processes, procedures, and resources to carry out organizational and management system activities

- Methods for measuring and evaluating performance

- Correction of problems and identification and implementation of opportunities for continuous improvement

- Management review of system performance, with feedback into the planning process[2]

The Case for Integration

The list of benefits to be realized by implementing management systems and consolidating common system requirements can be a long one. They can include:

- Alignment of business and QHSE goals and maximization of key performance indicators

- Recognition of how all people and processes interact and affect each other for more effective management of interfaces

- Creation of an integrated team approach focusing on mutual goals and benefits

- Establishment of common objectives, processes, and procedures

- Creation of synergies, thereby reducing redundancy and increasing effectiveness and efficiency

- Reduced risk through management based on factual data and overall analysis of performance metrics

- Systematic prioritization of effort for greatest organizational benefit

- Single framework for performance enhancement across all functional areas

- Comprehensive identification and analysis of problems and opportunities to improve

- Prevention of suboptimization—advancement of one area at the expense of another

- Increased understanding of all customers' and stakeholders' needs, wants, and perceptions

- Savings of time, money, and effort

- Establishment of accountability and clear boundaries

- Improved internal processes and communications[3]

And the list can go on and on. By establishing objectives and targets and then measuring progress against them, top management can ensure that the decisions and directions taken by the organization serve customer expectations and the strategic business goals of the organization. Clearly communicating the objectives and targets and establishing key performance indicators (KPI) that reflect them promotes understanding by the organization's personnel of the goals and how their activity and effort contributes toward achieving them. In other words, "I know how what I do around here contributes to the success of the company, which in turn garners me and my staff a continued paycheck." That's the bottom line for any business.

An effectively implemented integrated management system aligns policy with strategic and management system objectives and provides the framework upon which to translate these objectives into functional and personal targets. The goal-oriented framework depicted in the following diagram demonstrates how goals established at the uppermost levels of the organization flow down through the integrated management system to influence functional and personal objectives and targets.

Monitoring, measurement, and review activities, which are fundamental parts of most management systems, provide factual information upon which to make informed and prudent business decisions. Analysis of performance data allows

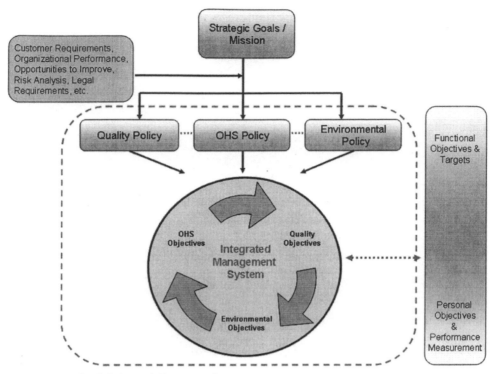

Figure 1.1. Goal-Oriented Framework

managers to gauge success in achieving objectives and to prioritize initiatives and activities based on where the greatest organizational benefit will be realized. Monitoring, measurement, and review processes provide input into the planning cycle, resulting in better decision-making, and, hopefully, reduced risk. Often, these processes can serve multiple system requirements. For example, a single means for carrying out and documenting corrective action to correct the root cause(s) of problems may be implemented with input coming from the quality, health and safety, and environmental management systems. This input can then be separated or viewed in total, depending upon the need. Logically, one might ask, why have different systems for managing different corrective actions? Still more relevant, why spend more money on different systems when one common system will do?

By far the most widely known international management system standard, ISO 9001:2000 describes a "process approach" for the development, implementation, and improvement of quality management systems. This approach recognizes that an organization is a system of processes and practices whereby the output of one process will likely form the input into another. While other standards may not specifically call for this approach, it is nonetheless one that can be effectively used to identify all the activities an organization needs to consider, including how they interface, and what controls must be put in place to ensure success and reduced risk.

In adopting this approach, all parties in the organization are able to recognize how people and processes interact and affect each other. Interfaces can be managed more effectively, and individuals develop an understanding of how their efforts contribute to the success or failure of their processes, or the processes of others.

Implementing and maintaining an integrated management system can provide the opportunity to identify and create synergies, thereby reducing redundancies, increasing effectiveness, and maximizing efficiencies. Establishing one set of processes and paperwork to accommodate the common areas of multiple systems reduces the overall size of the management system structure, reduces duplication and, in the end, reduces cost. And who's not concerned about reducing costs these days? Furthermore, when processes are created in isolation (or silos), the risk exists that measures designed to serve the best interests of one area may actually impact negatively upon another. An integrated, process-based approach prevents suboptimization and helps keep bureaucracy to a minimum, while at the same time enhancing system-based communication initiatives.

Typically, some of the core activities that fall within the "do" phase of the Plan-Do-Check-Act cycle are specific to one management system or another and may, therefore, need to be carried out and managed as such. However, the outputs of these activities may be fed through a common process for management review and subsequent organizational planning. This means that managers can take the "60,000 foot view," and by considering the needs and information produced by each system, make decisions that represent the greatest organizational benefit.[4]

Challenges to Integration

As is the case with any fundamental organizational change, the idea of integration does not come without its challenges. Unless top management actively leads and demonstrates real commitment to the integration effort, it is in danger of failing.

It is not unusual, however, for functional managers whose own systems are deemed to work well to feel threatened. The development, implementation, and maintenance of a management system are time-consuming, and frequent challenges can be encountered. Having gone through this process and reaching a point of comfort, functional heads in the areas of quality, health and safety, and environmental management could be forgiven for being reluctant to start another period of "storming."

On the other hand, these individuals are, by nature of their positions, generally comfortable with the concept of continuous improvement and champions for effective and efficient process management within their own disciplines. Top management must engage these key individuals and make it possible for all concerned to focus on the process rather than on comfort or ownership.

There are other challenges—sometimes real and sometimes perceived. Perhaps one of the most common fears encountered is the perception that defining processes and advocating consistency will stifle entrepreneurship, creativity, and flexibility. Also, historically, management systems were based on written procedures and a multitude of paperwork that ultimately increased bureaucracy and enforced controls that sometimes simply did not make sense. Perhaps on paper it made sense, but in the real world of day-to-day operations, challenges were seen and major obstacles were introduced.

The development of any new system carries with it certain costs. Likewise, integrating systems requires dedicated resources. If not well planned and implemented, the integrated system can quickly become a major cost area and a source of frustration. And if not managed well, the whole exercise of integrating management systems and processes can contribute to "turf wars" due to overlap or gaps.

One of the biggest decisions at the outset of the integration effort is whether to use internal resources or enlist the help of outsiders. If the choice is made to have the process remain within the company, and the person(s) tasked with designing the IMS are not completely competent and experienced in the management system and the requirements of the management system, the effort will often be plagued by false starts, unnecessary paperwork, inferior templates, and other outward indicators of inexperience. On the other hand, if a competent, external consultant is engaged, it is vital that both the credentials and the basic consulting philosophy of that consultant are well understood and aligned with the best interests of the organization. While anyone can hang a shingle, not all consultants are created equal. And without the requisite up-front work, the integration project can become a retirement fund. Translation—do your homework before hiring an integrated management systems consultant.

Even so, the business case for the integration effort is generally a strong one. With proper planning and focused effort, the efficiencies and savings to be realized from well-planned integration can far outweigh the up-front costs.

Consider the following example in which the audit and review processes of three management systems are combined for maximum benefit.

> ABC Company has three mature and well-established groups within the QHSE division. The quality, health and safety, and environmental groups each schedule and carry out a series of internal audits and compliance assessments. The results of these assessments are presented independently to upper management in formal management reviews. Also, internal auditors in each group are recruited and trained, with emphasis on their respective disciplines.
>
> ABC Company decides to integrate the auditing and management review activities. To do this, time and effort are required. Plans, procedures, schedules, and checklists must be revised. Auditors from each group must be trained in other areas of the integrated management system. Time must be taken from normal duties to accomplish these tasks.
>
> But once the up-front work has been done, the long-term benefits begin to be realized. Integrated schedules and checklists mean fewer audits. Cross-trained auditors can audit common management system elements together, thereby reducing the number of audits and freeing up more time for individual auditors and auditees alike. Management reviews may be reduced in number and increased in effectiveness. Factual information from each management system can be presented and considered together. Top management no longer views the information from each system in isolation but can more easily take the broader organizational view. Priorities can be established based truly on the areas of greatest organizational benefit, and QHSE objectives, targets, and goals can be aligned.

It is a common misconception that in order to develop and integrate management systems, businesses must restructure their processes and practices around the requirements of the guidelines or practices upon which the systems are based. This is not the case. Management systems have a greater chance of succeeding if they are created to reflect the way the organization actually does business. Rather than imposing procedures that don't quite fit and mandating the use of generic templates, organizations should instead undertake a gap analysis of existing practice and documents against the management system requirements. Once gaps in compliance and areas for improvement have been identified, a plan for implementation can be established and priorities can be set.

Systems Approach to Management

In the 1950s, quality guru W. Edwards Deming developed a continuous improvement model based on a sequence of four steps: Plan-Do-Study (Check)-Act. The "PDCA" cycle, also known as the Deming Wheel or the Deming Cycle, had its origin with the prominent statistician and Deming's mentor, Walter A. Shewhart, who introduced statistical process control at the Bell Laboratories in the 1920s. Deming expanded upon Shewhart's Plan-Do-See model and introduced process improvement and the continuous feedback loop.[5]

Using the PDCA cycle, individual processes are planned and carried out (PD). The results of those processes are checked and any action required to improve them is implemented (CA). Overall performance and results are analyzed and are fed back for consideration in the next planning phase.

Applied on an organizational level, the PDCA cycle allows management to view the organization as a system of processes that interact and influence one another. Managers plan based upon factual information gathered during the performance of work and analyze results in order to effect organizational improvements.

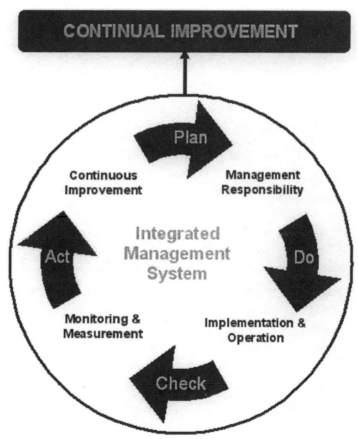

Figure 1.2. Management System PDCA Cycle for Continuous Improvement

Today's most commonly used management system frameworks are based to some degree upon variations of the PDCA cycle. System diagrams may vary somewhat from standard to standard, but all reflect the same PDCA system approach when defining management, implementation and operation, monitoring and measurement, and improvement activities.

Early models for management systems organized requirements in discreet elements. For example, until its 2000 version, the ISO 9001 international quality management system standard was comprised of twenty elements that were treated as individual activities and were generally managed and audited as such. As this type of management system model was put into use, it was recognized that successful organizations do not operate in silos. Various processes and functions affect each other. They do not necessarily operate independently, but they often affect each other. Nor do they work sequentially. Sometimes they take place simultaneously or cross over each other. More recent revisions of the popular standards mirror real-world organizational structure and flow, thus making them more applicable to the organizational processes they control. At the same time, the big hitters, including ISO 9001, ISO 14001, and OHSAS 18001 have been aligned with one another and all reflect the PDCA cycle. Current versions not only reflect how companies really work but also maintain a common framework, thus making it possible to more easily integrate them.

In the 1980s and 1990s the more commonly applied management system models were organized into elements. Key activities were treated as independent, and organizations often struggled to make their management system structures fit into the established frameworks of the chosen standards. In some ways the standards were, on the surface, discouraging the "silo mentality" while at the same time actually compelling their users to try to fragment their documentation and system controls into compartments.

As the use, application, and understanding of management systems grew, revisions to the standards mirrored that growth. The language of the standards changed to reflect the diversity of businesses seeking to apply them. It was recognized that whether they related to quality, health, safety, or environmental areas, the management systems were just that: management systems. The commonalities were identified, and the various standards began to align. Perhaps the most significant evolution was recognition of the fact that an organization does not (or perhaps more accurately, should not) operate in silos. Rather, they are a system of processes that often happen simultaneously and the output of one process forms the input into another.

Today's management system models are based upon a system- and process-based approach. The system approach identifies that effective management systems consist of several components. These include:

1. Identifying and meeting the needs and expectations of customers, stakeholders, and other interested parties

2. Developing policies, objectives, and targets required to help meet these needs and expectations

3. Implementing processes and defining the responsibilities needed to meet goals and objectives, to effectively carry out work, and minimize risk

4. Identifying and providing necessary resources

5. Establishing and applying measures to determine effectiveness and efficiency

6. Managing nonconformances and preventing recurrence by eliminating their causes

7. Identifying and implementing opportunities for improvement

Although the interpretation of these components may differ slightly depending upon the type of management system involved, the components themselves are always present.

For example, consider #1: Identifying and meeting the needs and expectations of customers, stakeholders, and other interested parties. For the quality management system the focus may be upon the end-use customer or the needs of the next department down the line of delivery. For the environmental management system, the definition of the customer expands to include regulators, the community, and those potentially affected by environmental issues. For the health and safety system, the primary focus becomes the protection of the internal customer and those working under the influence of the management system processes. In all cases, customer focus is the overlying principle. Organizationally, a system must be in place to identify the customers, stakeholders, or interested parties, to define and achieve their expectations and, where possible, to implement improvements to better serve their interests.

Each management system within the integrated framework has its own requirements, particularly within the "do" phase. But, there are always common areas, and these serve as the basis for integration.

INTEGRATED MANAGEMENT SYSTEMS: PRACTICAL APPLICATIONS

A t the core of the integrated management system are the requirements of all constituent systems that can be managed together (e.g., management review). Next are those that are common to two systems and can be carried out together (e.g., task risk assessment). Finally, there are those that are specific to individual systems. All are supported by common organizational processes and reflect overall goals and objectives. The outputs of all management system processes are considered when implementing improvements and planning and determining resource requirements.

It is important to remember that in order to be integrated, components must logically fit together and must be managed together. Merely putting procedures from various systems into one master document file does not equal integration. True integration ties all components of the organization into one coherent system where all activities, whether implemented together or individually, are focused on achievement of overall goals and are ultimately the guiding mission of the organization.

At its most evolved state, an integrated management system would see managers taking care of a range of functions within their area of responsibility. A common example is the QHSE department, wherein quality assurance/quality control, health and safety, environmental management, and even security have processes in common and are managed together within the umbrella of the QHSE management system to serve organizational goals and objectives.

Common Requirements of Management System Standards

As discussed, integration logically begins with the elements that are common to all of the applied management systems. In the following QHSE example, the common elements carry through the quality, health and safety, and environmental

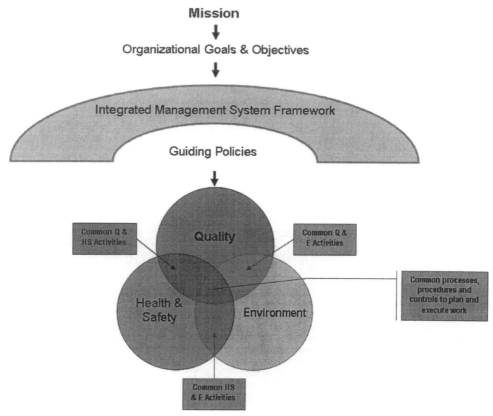

Figure 2.1. Integration Model for HSEQ Systems

management systems and support the specific requirements of each individual system within the integrated framework.

ISO Guide 72 identifies a number of common elements that exist among most management systems and that can be arranged under six main subject areas:

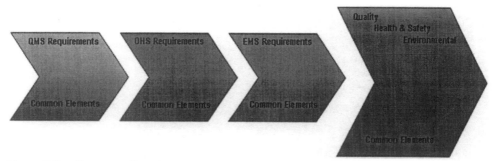

Figure 2.2. Common Requirements as the Basis for Integration

1. Policy

2. Planning

3. Implementation and Operation

4. Performance Assessment

5. Improvement

6. Management Review

This structure reflects the process approach to the PDCA model and is used by writers of various standards and guidelines to organize requirements into a common set of activities. Within each of the subject areas, similar management system requirements can be addressed.[1]

PLAN

Policy

Quality, health and safety, and environmental management standards share a requirement that top management define the overall policy with respect to the management system. This policy should demonstrate the organization's commitment, reflect the mission of the organization, and provide a framework for setting objectives and targets.

The policy must:

- Be appropriate to the activities, products, and services of the organization

- Include a commitment to comply with the requirements of the management system, including relevant legal and other requirements to which the organization subscribes

- Include a commitment to continually improve

- Provide a framework for establishing and reviewing objectives

- Be communicated and understood by all persons working within the organization

- Be reviewed at regular intervals to ensure continuing suitability

Policies for quality, health and safety, and environmental management may be separate or incorporated into one overall HSEQ policy. Whichever approach is taken, the process by which management develops the policies, reviews them, and communicates them is the same. Area-specific policies should be compatible with the nature and intent of the overall policy.[2]

Planning

To be effective and to improve, all organizations must plan and prioritize. In the planning phase, organizational objectives and targets are set, risk is evaluated, legal and other relevant requirements are considered, past performance is measured, and opportunities for improvement are identified. During the planning phase, the following common activities take place.

Objectives and Targets

Clear objectives and targets must be established for an effectively functioning integrated management system. They must be realistic, measurable, and consistent with the overlying policy. They must take into account legal and other requirements, including those of customers and identified stakeholders, risks, results of past performance, and the outcome of management review. Objectives and targets must be set at all relevant functional levels, measured, and modified as needed to reflect changes. In addition to these common characteristics, specific management system objectives may also address other requirements. For example, environmental management system objectives and targets must take into account environmental aspects and impacts that could possibly impact the organization's public relations image.

Aspects, Impacts, and Risks

The organization must identify the aspects of its activities, products, services, or locations that relate to the management system, evaluate the risk associated with them, and consider them when setting objectives and establishing, implementing, and managing the management system. Within the environmental management system, the organization would be expected to identify the environmental aspects that could potentially impact upon the environment and over which the organization has control. In the area of health and safety, the organization would take appropriate steps to identify hazards and risks to people. Under the quality management system, the organization would consider risks to organizational performance, including finance, scheduling, and customer satisfaction. Again, while the application of the overall requirement may differ, the aspects, impacts, and risks can be determined, documented, managed, and reviewed in common, as they often overlap.

When addressing risks, more and more organizations are developing comprehensive risk management strategies that bring all forms of risk identification and management under one umbrella. For instance, rather than developing separate means for ranking risks in different areas, an overall organizational risk-ranking process and matrix may be put in place with consideration given to significant risk areas such as people, environment, assets, production, regulatory compliance, public perception, etc. Likewise, risk identification and controls at the task level may be common to two or more systems. For instance, on the job site, task risk assessments and toolbox talks would cover not only health and safety risk-reduction measures but also those associated with environmental aspects and their potential impact.

Identification of Legal and Other Requirements

The organization must identify and have access to legal and other relevant requirements to which it subscribes relating to its products, activities, or services. These requirements must be considered when planning and implementing the management system and the activities of the organization. An inherent aspect of all management systems is the requirement for them to comply. Examples of legal or other requirements would be a relevant industry code or an OHS regulation.

Organization Structure, Roles, Responsibilities, and Authority

In order for the organization to be effective, it is necessary that people understand their roles, responsibilities, and authorities in relation to their job functions and the management system. Top management must define and document these roles and their interrelationship and communicate them within the organization.

The various management system standards all identify the need for a management representative who, irrespective of other duties, has the defined responsibility and authority to ensure that the management system is established, implemented, and maintained in accordance with the relevant standard and who reports to the top management team on system performance and opportunities for improvement. Where two or more systems are integrated, the management representative may represent the interests of all systems.

Contingency Planning/Emergency Preparedness

The organization must establish processes and procedures to identify and respond to potential or actual emergencies, accidents, or disasters. Procedures must be established to prevent or mitigate the consequences of such occurrences, taking into consideration such things as safety of personnel, potential environmental impacts, and continuity of business operations. Emergency response programs and exercises may effectively cover unplanned events of any type.[3]

DO

Implementation and Operation

Operational controls and product and service realization processes must be established and carried out under specified conditions to meet objectives and satisfy requirements. While all management systems require these controls, it is typically in this area that the systems will diverge and activities and procedures specific to the individual management system will be required. However, it is still important to remember that processes seldom take place in isolation, and the failure to effectively carry out a process specific to one management system may still influence the success of a process in another area. Likewise, failures in different areas may have a common result.

For example, within the health and safety management system, great care may be taken to manage behaviors and conditions that could result in harm to people. The same care may be taken within the environmental management system to manage aspects that could have significant negative impact upon the environment. But, if the procedures or equipment that is managed through the quality manage-

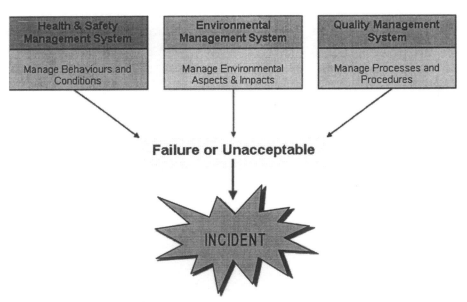

Figure 2.3. Example of Potential Common Impact of Failure Within Individual Systems

ment system are not effective, an incident that causes damage to people or the environment is still inevitable.

During the implementation and operation phase there are also shared requirements. Like those in other phases, common processes and procedures may be established to control and implement them.

Resource Management

Infrastructure and environment The organization must determine, provide, and maintain the infrastructure needed to achieve its objectives, ensure product conformity (quality), and protect its people (health and safety) and the environment (environment). This includes buildings, equipment, tools, work spaces, utilities, and supporting services such as transportation or communication. It must also provide a suitable working environment in which people can work to their, and the organization's, best advantage. Failure to provide any one of these could potentially result in nonconformances, delays, additional cost, or harm to people or the environment.

Human resources All management systems are dependent upon the competency of the people who work within them; therefore, it is important that the organization defines the required competencies associated with the work being performed and ensures that people carrying out that work have those competencies. A distinction has been made between "competency" and "qualification," recognizing that a person may possess the required paper qualifications to occupy a position but may not necessarily be competent to do the job. Competency is a combination of education, training, skills, and experience in a particular job or task. It may be attained through formal education, training external to the organization, internal instruction, on-the-job training, or a combination of these and other means.

Within the human resources function, processes may be instituted that address the requirements of several standards. This would typically include processes to:

- Identify core and QHSE competencies associated with a position (e.g., job descriptions)

- Hire and provide indoctrination to new employees

- Identify requirements for competency enhancement and provide training or take other appropriate action

- Maintain records of competency and training

- Evaluate the effectiveness of training or other action taken to achieve competence

- Evaluate performance

Policies, procedures, and processes for human resource management are generally applicable to all management systems. For example, training matrixes may identify core job-related skills as well as health and safety, regulatory, environmental, and other training.[4]

Documentation and Records

All management systems require documents, and all require records. To understand these requirements, it is necessary to first understand the difference between a management system "document" and a "record." The guiding policies, procedures, checklists, and forms that make up the system are defined as "documents." Records provide historical information of performance. For instance, the blank version of a form is a management system "document." When the form is filled in, it becomes a "record."

One of the most common problems associated with building a management system is the tendency to overdocument. Recent versions of standards such as ISO 9001:2000 (ISO 9001:2008) have become less prescriptive in their documentation requirements, leaving it largely to the user to determine what level of documentation is required to maintain effective control and to continuously improve.

Most management systems are, however, fairly consistent in that their basic documentation structures usually include:

- Policy statement(s)

- Objectives and targets

- Manual or a similar document setting forth strategy or policy

- Procedures for key management system areas

- Additional procedures or work instructions deemed necessary by the organization to maintain effective control

- Flowcharts, forms, checklists, and other supporting documents

- Records[5]

A typical management system document hierarchy can be depicted by a classic pyramid example.

Document and data control Management system documents and data must be controlled. Once established, processes and infrastructures for document and data control will serve multiple management systems. These must include controls to:

- Approve documents for adequacy prior to use

- Review, update, and reapprove documents when necessary

- Identify changes and revision status

- Make relevant versions of documents available at all points of use

- Ensure that documents are legible, identifiable, and accessible

- Ensure that documents of external origin are identified and distribution controlled

- Identify and prevent unintended use of obsolete documents

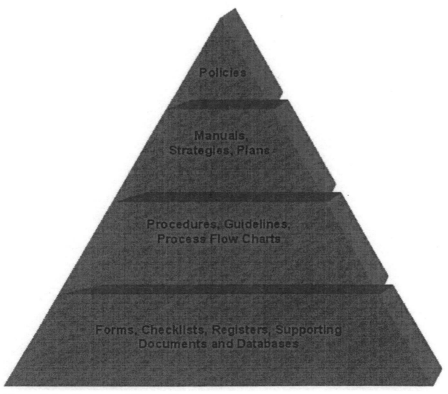

Figure 2.4.   Document Pyramid

Master lists and master document files are fast becoming replaced by electronic databases with restricted access and electronic signatures (see the chapter on management systems and IT solutions). This is an effective way to ensure that revision control is maintained and that current versions are available at all times. Where electronic document management systems are put in place, regular backups become a key requirement for records management.

Records management   As is the case with document and data control processes, procedures for records management are also common to all management systems. Once established, records management practices can accommodate all information, regardless of source. Requirements for records management call for the establishment, implementation, and maintenance of controls for the identification, storage, protection, retrieval, retention, and disposal of records. A records matrix is a helpful tool when defining records controls.[6]

All management system models require procedures for document and data control and records management. Documents and records can be in any form or media. Therefore, arrangements must be made to control and protect both hard copy and electronic documents and records in whatever format they may be produced. One suite of procedures will serve different management systems. Depending upon the complexity of the organization's documents and records, any number of procedures may be needed, but they will generally include:

- Document identification and numbering

- Approving, issuing, and revising documents (including revision control)

- Control of documents of external origin (including standards, codes, and other legal documents)

- Design document control

- Supplier document control

- Records management procedure

- Control and backup of electronic records

- Disaster recovery plan

Communication

Mechanisms for communications, both within the organization and with external parties, can be designed to accommodate all management system requirements. Authorities for communication may differ from system to system. For example, one party may be tasked with media communication, another with

Table 2.1. Sample Basic Records Matrix (partial)

Record Type	Responsible	Identification Method	Paper Storage	Electronic Storage	Handling	Retention Period	Disposal Authority
HR Files	HR Manager	Alphabetical, by name	Locked cabinet, HR office	HR drive, controlled access, BU daily	No special requirements	1 year following completion of contract	General Manager (shred)
Data Recordings	IT Technician	Numerical, by date	Fireproof cabinet, IT office, off-site vault	Main server, BU server	Fireproof, waterproof container	30 days	IT Manager
Audit Files	HSEQ Manager	Audit Number	Locked cabinet, HSE office	Shared HSEQ drive, general read-only access	Considered "company confidential"	3 years	HSEQ Manager

communication with regulators, and another with internal communications; however, all persons and departments within the organization share the processes for communication and the means by which communication takes place. At a minimum, organizations must establish the means to communicate internally among the various levels and functions of the organization as well as methods to receive and respond to communications, including complaints from customers and other interested external parties.

The first step is to implement the means for communication. Examples can include electronic mail, bulletin boards, meeting structures, newsletters, intranet, forums, information sessions, or whatever other means are appropriate. The next step is to ensure that these mechanisms are effectively put into use and that the information gathered is funneled into the overall management process.

Supplier Management and Purchasing

While not all management system models explicitly state a requirement related to supplier management and purchasing, this is, nonetheless, an important and common area of consideration. Of particular interest is contractor safety management, especially if your staff and contractors are to be performing work or similar high-risk tasks in the same location or in close proximity to your own workers.

Supplier management   ISO 9000 includes *mutually beneficial supplier relationships* in the eight management principles upon which a quality system is built. This serves to recognize that suppliers of critical goods and services that potentially impact upon the deliverable to the customer or upon key internal processes are vitally important to the organization's overall success. It also recognizes that it is not always practical to eliminate potential suppliers if their performance has not been satisfactory. Sometimes there is only one supplier or the customer or intercompany relationships dictate the use of a certain supplier. In these cases, processes must be established to ensure effective control over the product or service being supplied or to help the supplier to improve. So, having established that mutually beneficial supplier relationships will help ensure quality, it is not a big step to apply the same philosophy to the areas of health and safety or environmental protection. It is equally important that suppliers whose people, product, or performance can impact upon HSE also have appropriate HSE processes in place or are trained in, and perform within, the contracting organization's own processes. Contractor safety management is a key example here. Therefore, processes for supplier management can be deemed to be a common management system requirement, although they may at certain times be applied slightly differently.

Purchasing   ISO 9001 requires that organizations have processes for defining and documenting purchasing requirements, including those for quality (e.g., inspections, test certificates, etc.). Essentially, if the specification is not clear to the supplier, the product or service provided may not be acceptable. Purchasing documents should also state any applicable HSE requirements. For example, in the case of coveralls, the purchase agreement will stipulate the number, quantity, and size of the coveralls as well as the applicable fire rating, color, and markings. Hence, the single system for controlling purchases is applicable to the quality, health and safety, and environmental management systems.[7]

CHECK

Performance Assessment

In the Plan-Do-Check-Act model for management systems, the third cycle calls for monitoring and measurement to determine the extent to which requirements are being met. Information is recorded to track performance of operational controls and to evaluate the ability of those controls to achieve the planned results. Information is also recorded to evaluate achievement of objectives and compliance with various management system requirements.

Monitoring and Measuring

Monitoring and measurement of processes and their output (products) is fundamental to any system and necessary in every department. Product inspections and tests, calibrations, design reviews, OHS inspections, service performance checklists, and verifications of calculations are all examples of monitoring and measurement activities. The outputs of these activities provide vital information that, although gathered from independent means, is directed through a common process of assessment in which the information is considered in its totality to provide an indicator of organizational performance and health.

At the ground level, there are often many opportunities to integrate monitoring and measuring activities to meet the needs of two or more systems. Common inspection activities and reports, checklists, and personnel assignment all aid in the integration of effort.

Compliance Evaluation

Organizations are required to evaluate compliance to the legal and other requirements to which they subscribe. Compliance evaluations are specific to the particular discipline; however, the system by which they are scheduled, carried out, documented, and input into management review can be common. The controls instituted to ensure compliance could also be common. Likewise, where practical, compliance assessments can sometimes be carried out by the same individuals at the same time where one area is subject to multiple regulatory or legal requirements and where compliance auditors are competent to assess those multiple requirements.

Internal Audit

As discussed earlier, the requirement for self-assessment is integral to the continuous improvement aspect of any management system. Audits determine whether or not the management system(s) conforms to the requirements of the standards and specifications to which the organization subscribes, has been effectively implemented and maintained, and is being complied with. Audits must be conducted, based upon the status and importance of the activity, the significance of the management system aspects, areas of risk, organizational performance, and the results of previous audits. They must be carried out by auditors who are objective and impartial—in other words, auditors should not audit their own work.

There is no need to have separate audit schedules, plans, reports, and audit management. In fact, this can lead to scheduling issues, redundancies, and time-management issues. Integration of the auditing function provides a bigger bang for the auditing buck. Plans, procedures, schedules, and checklists can be developed to meet multiple requirements. Since auditing protocols are basically the same regardless of the standard to which the audit is being conducted, auditors can be trained in auditing techniques and cross-trained in the requirements of the applicable management system requirements.

When integrated audits are performed, the audit report presents factual information spanning more than one management system. This means that management no longer views the performance information from each system in isolation. Actions arising from the integrated management systems audit can be more effectively prioritized to ensure that efforts are focused on areas of greatest organizational benefit and impact upon overall objectives, targets, and goals.

Nonconformance Control and Opportunities for Improvement

One of the key activities at the heart of any formalized management system is the identification and rectification of nonconformances. Although the wording may differ, all of the recognized standards require that nonconformances be identified and corrected, and that action be taken to mitigate their impact. It has been customary for nonconformance reporting among quality, health and safety, and environmental management systems to be carried out separately; however, this need not be the case.

Simply defined, a nonconformance is a failure to meet a specified requirement. That being the case, nonconformances can be identified in any area. While they

HSEQ Report Card

Card Number:	Date:
Title:	
Reference:	

HSE	☐ Incident ☐ Near Miss ☐ Hazard ☐ Suggestion
QUALITY	☐ Nonconformance ☐ Opportunity for Improvement

Describe the issue or opportunity

Describe immediate action taken / suggested or the potential consequences

Follow-up

CAR #_____   Incident #_____   None Required ☐

Signature:

Figure 2.5.   Sample Report Card (HSE and Quality)

may be termed "hazards," "near misses," or "incidents" in the HSE system, these failures are still nonconformances.

In recent years, some organizations have moved toward developing a common set of forms and processes to identify and to take action on nonconformances and opportunities for improvement across several management systems. In the analysis process (also a requirement of formalized management systems), the type and nature of the issues can then be analyzed and comprehensive management reports can be prepared. One area that has significantly changed is the way in which technology is used to simplify these processes.[8]

ACT

Continual Improvement

Effective control is the outcome of a properly functioning management system. The next step is continual improvement, and this is where the management system can pay the greatest dividends.

For many years, standards such as ISO 9001 have carried an implied requirement for continual improvement. With no explicitly stated requirement, organizations holding registrations or claiming compliance could theoretically meet the minimum requirements of the standards year after year, showing no marked effort toward continual improvement. But standards are just minimums—particularly international standards that must be applicable in so many different countries and environments. It hardly benefits any organization to continually meet the minimum. Furthermore, management systems cost money, and it is when they are used to drive continual improvement that they pay for themselves several times over.

Many of today's common or well-known management systems are very clear in their requirements for continual improvement, and the process-based models include several requirements that ensure that improvement takes place. Indeed, measuring progress against established objectives is the whole basis for today's management systems and that one characteristic will, in and of itself, drive improvement.

Through the use of their policies, objectives, targets, audit results, feedback from customers and interested parties, analysis of performance data, corrective action, preventive action, and management review, organizations will improve their performance and ultimately, their bottom lines.

Corrective Action

Nonconformance control helps catch and correct problems. Corrective action delves into the root cause(s) of those problems—why they happened in the first place. A common mistake when implementing management systems is to require that every nonconformance have root-cause correction completed. Some issues are quite simply one-time events, and the time and effort taken to identify and eliminate the root cause(s) is time wasted. On the other hand, recurring problems or those that are critical and must not be repeated warrant investigation and root-cause correction, appropriate to the risks encountered.

The corrective action control process, forms, and management can and should be common to all management systems within an organization. This allows all issues to be considered together to ensure that priorities are established and that focus is given to those issues that represent the largest overall risk and/or return. Furthermore, the consequence of a significant issue is seldom restricted to one area. For instance, a quality issue can create a potential danger to people or the environment. An integrated approach toward root-cause investigation and corrective action, regardless of which system actually identified the issue, ensures that all impacts are given due consideration.

Corrective action logs, forms, teams, reviews, databases, and statistics should be integrated in order to make the greatest organizational impact.

Preventive Action

Whereas corrective action is reactive in nature, preventive action is proactive. It is the preventive action process that truly saves time, money, lives, and the environment. Catching and eliminating potential problems before they occur is obviously the most effective control that can be put in place. As is the case with the corrective action controls, those established for preventive action should be integrated. In fact, it is normal for the corrective action and preventive action processes to work together with common forms, databases, measurement, and resource allocations. This is a sensible approach. When judging whether an action is preventive in nature, the first question might be: "Is this proactive, or reactive to something that occurred?" If the latter, it is corrective.

In the quality world, if a nonconformance occurred, the action taken to address the root cause is corrective. If a nonconformance occurred, the action taken to ensure that it does not happen again is also corrective. If a nonconformance has not yet occurred, action taken to avoid one is preventive.

In the HSE world, action taken to address the root cause of an incident or accident is corrective. Action taken to address the root cause of a near miss is also corrective since it is in response to an actual occurrence. Action taken to eliminate a hazard is preventive.

With elimination being the optimal means of hazard or nonconformance control, the corrective and preventive action processes are two of the most important in management system structures. The requirement for corrective and preventive action is common to all systems, and the methods and documents may also be managed in common.

Management Review

It might be said that the Plan-Do-Check-Act cycle starts and ends with management review. It is, arguably, the single-most important element of any management system. Through the management review process, committed leaders, acting upon factual information from the management systems, make informed decisions and identify the resources required to enable the organization to run efficiently, safely, and without damage to the environment.

Management review must take place at regular intervals to ensure the continuing suitability, adequacy, and effectiveness of the various management systems. Information gathered from various sources is analyzed and used to plan for the organization and to assess opportunities for improvement.

Health and safety, environmental, and quality management standards are consistent in their required inputs to management review. These must include, but should not be limited to:

- Results of audits, inspections, and assessments

- Feedback from customers and interested parties

- Performance data from various processes and systems (e.g., nonconformances, HSE statistics, etc.)

- Results of evaluations of compliance to legal and other requirements

- Status of corrective and preventive actions

- Changes that may affect the organization, including new legal or other requirements related to aspects and related risks

- Follow-up actions from previous management reviews

- Recommendations for improvement

Outputs from management review include decisions and actions necessary to improve the effectiveness of the organizational controls and the management system(s), improvements related to the requirements of the customer or other interested parties, and resources needed to enable improvement to take place.

Management reviews are documented, and action items may be managed within the integrated management system. The information that is input into management review is considered and used to plan—thus completing the Plan-Do-Check-Act cycle and starting it once again.[9]

MANAGEMENT SYSTEMS:
SAFETY LEADS THE WAY (FINALLY)

Although there are currently formal international standards for managing quality (ISO 9001:2000–9001:2008) and the environment (ISO 14001:2004), there is currently no universally recognized International Organization Standardization (ISO) certifiable standard for occupational health and safety management, although it has not been for a lack of trying. It has been suggested that ISO has been wary of becoming involved in occupational health and safety, for a number of reasons. At an ISO workshop in 1996, it was concluded that the time was "not right" for an occupational health and safety management standard, based on the feedback of participants. In 2000, ISO rejected an approach from the International Labour Organization (ILO) with respect to an international standard on occupational health and safety management systems.

During this process, and after the International Labour Organization reviewed over twenty different national occupational health and safety management system models, the ILO decided to develop their own noncertifiable guidance document. The *Guidelines on Occupational Safety and Health Management Systems* was published by the ILO-OSH in 2001. Although there has been discussion that the ILO does not intend to make the standard certifiable, the Chinese government has adopted the ILO system and has used it to develop a certification framework.

On the international stage, the increasing pressure by business and government agencies to ensure effective mechanisms for reporting on performance and demonstrating corporate responsibility, coupled with the popularity of ISO 9001:2000 (9001:2008) and ISO 14001:2004, has led to a growing interest in the occupational health and safety management system standard, OHSAS 18001.[1]

OSHA's 18001:2007: A New OH&S Management System Standard

In the absence of an official ISO standard, OHSAS 18001 is considered by some to be a leading management system standard for occupational health and safety management. International certification bodies and national standards bodies in the United Kingdom, Ireland, South Africa, Spain, and Malaysia are using OHSAS 18001 for certification purposes, and it is estimated that organizations in some eighty countries have adopted OHSAS 18001. OHSAS 18001:2007 now refers to itself as a standard, not a specification or document, as in earlier editions. It's been noted that this reflects the increasing adoption of OHSAS 18001 as the basis for national standards on occupational health and safety management systems.[2]

ILO Guidelines for OH&S Management System: An International Opportunity

In an introductory statement on the *Guidelines on Occupational Safety and Health Management Systems*, it is noted that the guidelines were prepared on the basis of a broad-based approach involving the ILO and its tripartite constituents and other stakeholders. They have been shaped by internationally agreed occupational safety and health principles as defined in relevant international labor standards. Consequently, they provide a unique and powerful instrument for the development of a sustainable safety structure and culture within the business community. The guidelines on OSH management systems were developed by the International Labour Organization (ILO) according to internationally agreed principles defined by the ILO's tripartite constituents. This tripartite approach provided the strength, flexibility, and appropriate basis for the development of a sustainable safety culture through the practical application of the guidelines. The ILO voluntary guidelines on OSH management systems reflect ILO values and instruments relevant to the protection of workers' safety and health, based on their approach to worker safety and protection.

To help profile the practical application of the ILO guidelines, the following overview of some of the main aspects of the guidelines on OSH management systems is intended to profile clarity. As you read this section, try to take a moment to conduct a gap analysis in your head (or better still, on paper or in a spreadsheet) of the sections and features that complement your current management system, or that differ greatly. Also look for similarities between your current management system for environmental and quality management and see if you can identify opportunities for improvement based on the ILO model and your current management system structure.

ILO Guidelines on OSH Management Systems

The following is a summary overview of the key features of the *ILO Guidelines for Occupational Safety and Health Management Systems*.

Objectives
1. A national framework for occupational safety and health management systems
   a. National policy
   b. National guidelines
   c. Tailored guidelines
2. The occupational safety and health management system in the organization
   a. Occupational safety and health policy
   b. Worker participation
   c. Organizing
      (1) Responsibility and accountability
      (2) Competence and training
      (3) Occupational safety and health management system documentation
      (4) Communication
   d. Planning and implementation
      (1) Initial review
      (2) System planning, development, and implementation
      (3) Occupational safety and health objectives
      (4) Hazard prevention
         (a) Prevention and control measures
         (b) Management of change
         (c) Emergency prevention, preparedness, and response
         (d) Procurement
         (e) Contracting
   e. Evaluation
      (1) Performance monitoring and measurement
      (2) Investigation of work-related injuries, ill health, diseases, and incidents and their impact on safety and health performance
      (3) Audit
      (4) Management review
   f. Action for improvement
      (1) Preventive and corrective action
      (2) Continual improvement[3]

Objectives

The mandate of the objective-setting process is to provide a framework that should help contribute to the protection of workers from hazards and to the elimination of work-related injuries, ill health, diseases, incidents, and deaths.

For any organization, the guidelines are intended to provide guidance regarding the integration of OSH management-system elements in the organization as a component of policy and management arrangements and to motivate the organization, particularly employers, owners, managerial staff, workers, and their representatives in applying appropriate OSH management principles and methods to continually improve OSH performance.

The Occupational Safety and Health Management System in the Organization

Occupational safety and health, including compliance with the OSH requirements pursuant to national laws and regulations, are the responsibility and duty of the employer. The employer should show strong leadership and commitment to OSH activities in the organization and make appropriate arrangements for the establishment of an OSH management system. The system should contain the main elements of policy, organizing, planning and implementation, evaluation, and action for improvement.

Occupational Safety and Health Policy

The ILO guidelines suggest the employer, in consultation with workers and their representatives, should set out in writing an OSH policy that should be:

- specific to the organization and appropriate to its size and the nature of its activities

- concise, clearly written, dated, and made effective by the signature or endorsement of the employer or the most senior accountable person in the organization

- communicated and readily accessible to all persons at their place of work and reviewed for continuing suitability

- made available to relevant external interested parties, as appropriate

At a minimum, the OSH policy should include the following key principles and objectives:

- protecting the safety and health of all members of the organization by preventing work-related injuries, ill health, diseases, and incidents

- complying with relevant OSH laws and regulations, voluntary programs, collective agreements on OSH, and other requirements to which the organization subscribes

- ensuring that workers and their representatives are consulted and encouraged to participate actively in all elements of the OSH management system

- continually improve the performance of the OSH management system

Consistent with the focus of this book, the ILO guidelines suggest the OSH management systems should be compatible with, or integrated in, other management systems in the organization. With increased globalization and attempts at the rationalization of safety and legislating of worker-health issues among countries, this integration and rationalization is fast becoming the mantra of many in the international, health, safety, quality, and environmental management community.

Worker Participation

Consistent with Z1000 in Canada and OHSAS 18001:2007, worker participation is considered to be an essential element of the OSH management system.

Employers are encouraged to ensure workers and their safety and health representatives are consulted, informed, and trained on all aspects of OSH, including emergency arrangements associated with their work. The employer is recommended to make arrangements for workers and their safety and health representatives to have the time and resources to participate actively in the safety management system. Participation drives ownership, and some degree of ownership is an integral part of any management system.

In Canada, many jurisdictions have mandated this participation through legislated involvement in the occupational health and safety committee/representative process, entrenching in regulations the right to be involved in discussions and decisions having the potential to impact worker health and safety.

Under the focus in the ILO safety management system guidelines, the employer should ensure, as appropriate, the establishment and efficient functioning of a safety and health committee in accordance with laws and practice. Of course, functioning *effectively* is a key to this requirement.

Organizing: Responsibility

The ILO guidelines suggest the employer should have overall responsibility for the protection of workers' safety and health and provide leadership for OSH activities in the organization. This is not inconsistent with the view that those who are the "directing minds of the organization" not only control the organization, including business objectives, but also their management systems. This is a key aspect of the internal responsibility system for management system accountability that we will profile later.

Part of the obligation of maintaining this responsibility includes the intelligent and rational provision of resources. ILO guidelines require the employer and senior management to allocate responsibility, accountability, and authority for the development, implementation, and performance of the OSH management system and the achievement of the relevant OSH objectives. Further emphasis is mandated for the structures and processes that should be established, including:

- ensuring that OSH is a line-management responsibility that is known and accepted at all levels

- defining and communicating to the members of the organization the responsibility, accountability, and authority of persons who identify, evaluate, or control OSH hazards and risks

- providing effective supervision, as necessary, to ensure the protection of workers' safety and health

- promoting cooperation and communication among members of the organization, including workers and their representatives, to implement the elements of the organization's OSH management system

- fulfilling the principles of OSH management systems contained in relevant national guidelines, tailored guidelines, or voluntary programs, as appropriate, to which the organization subscribes

- establishing and implementing a clear OSH policy and measurable objectives

- establishing effective arrangements to identify and eliminate or control work-related hazards and risks and promoting health at work

- establishing prevention and health promotion programs

- ensuring effective arrangements for the full participation of workers and their representatives in the fulfillment of the OSH policy

Accountability

The requirements for organizing the occupational health and safety management system are consistent with the other management systems profiled in this book. Added emphasis is placed on the level of participation it is felt workers need in order to be able to positively contribute to the safety management process. Specifically, the guidelines require that appropriate resources be provided to ensure that those responsible for OSH, including the safety and health committee, can perform their functions properly. Also, effective arrangements for the full participation of workers and their representatives in safety and health committees should be facilitated.

Similar to ISO 9001:2000 (and 2008), ISO 14001:2004, CSA Z1000-06 in Canada, and ANSI/AIHA Z10-2005 in the United States, the ILO guidelines require a person or persons at the senior management level be appointed, where appropriate, with responsibility, accountability, and authority for the development, implementation and periodic review and evaluation of the OSH management system, periodic reporting to the senior management on the performance of the OSH management system, and promotion of the participation of all members of the organization in the OHS management system.

Competence and Training

When considering an integrated approach to competence, awareness, and training, emphasis should be placed on initiatives that demonstrate documented evidence of the effectiveness of the competence model.

The ILO guidelines require that necessary OSH competence requirements be defined by the employer and arrangements established and maintained to ensure that all persons are competent to carry out the safety and health aspects of their duties and responsibilities.

Typical training requirements reference the expectation that training cover all members of the organization (as appropriate), be conducted by competent persons, provide effective and timely initial and refresher training at appropriate intervals, include participants' evaluation of their comprehension and retention of the training, and that it be reviewed periodically.

The emphasis on worker participation in this business process suggests the review should include the safety and health committee; however, in a practical sense, it's been the experience of the authors that most organizations do not leave the job of training and competence verification to a joint worker-and-management committee, except for general discussions of a nonstrategic nature. Those committees who do take ownership of this process are, it's suggested, the exception rather than the rule.

Occupational Safety and Health Management System Documentation

Depending on the size and nature of the organization, the OSH management system documentation should be established and maintained consistently with the

OSH policy and objectives of the organization. As with any business, the ability to achieve objectives and targets should be rationalized based on the realities of the business environment, including regulatory realities, market forces, and availability of competent resources. Under the ILO guidelines, the occupational safety and health management system in the organization should ensure the following:

- the allocated key OSH management roles and responsibilities for the implementation of the OSH management system

- the significant OSH hazards/risks arising from the organization's activities and the arrangements for their prevention and control

- arrangements, procedures, instructions, or other internal documents used within the framework of the OSH management system

Section 3.5.2 of the ILO guidelines deals with the record and documentation requirements of the management system. Specifically, there is an expectation for management system documentation to be clearly written and presented in a way that is understood by those who have to use it and periodically reviewed, revised as necessary, communicated, and readily accessible to all appropriate or affected members of the organization. See ISO 9001 and 14001 for similar exemptions.

The establishment, management, and maintenance of records should be developed locally and according to the needs of the organization. This is where many organizations default to the ISO 9001 quality management system requirement (where this is one) and use their policy or procedure for control of documents and records to cover their health, safety, and environmental management system documentation, and record requirements as well.

The ILO guidelines require that documents and records should be identifiable and traceable, and their retention times should be specified. Additionally, workers should have the right to access records relevant to their working environment and health, while respecting the need for confidentiality.

There are a number of different types of records typically maintained by a safety management system, and the ILO guidelines identify some common examples, including:

- records arising from the implementation of the OSH management system

- records of work-related injuries, ill health, diseases, and incidents

- records arising from local or national laws, or regulations dealing with OSH

- records of workers' exposures, surveillance of the working environment, and workers' health

- the results of both active and reactive monitoring

Communication

The ILO guidelines place importance on the value of communication in the effectiveness of the health and safety management system. Arrangements and procedures should be established and maintained for:

- receiving, documenting, and responding appropriately to internal and external communications related to OSH

- ensuring the internal communication of OSH information among relevant levels and functions of the organization

- ensuring that the concerns, ideas, and inputs of workers and their representatives on OSH matters are received, considered, and responded to

Planning and Implementation

One of the most critical aspects of any management system is the strategic plan defined for its successful execution. The guidelines suggest that the OSH management system and relevant arrangements should be evaluated by an initial review. In the case where there is no OSH management system, or if the organization is new, it's suggested that the initial review should serve as a basis for establishing the OSH management system.

Guidance suggests that the initial review should be carried out by competent persons in consultation with workers and/or their representatives, as appropriate. Ideally, the review should:

- identify the current applicable local or national laws and regulations, national guidelines, tailored guidelines, voluntary programs, and other requirements to which the organization subscribes

- identify, anticipate, and assess hazards and risks to safety and health arising from the existing or proposed work environment and work organization

- determine whether planned or existing controls are adequate to eliminate hazards or control risks

- analyze the data provided from workers' health surveillance

As with any formal management review process, the results of any initial review should be documented, become the basis for making decisions regarding the implementation of the OSH management system, and provide a baseline from which continual improvement of the organization's OSH management system can be measured.

System Planning, Development, and Implementation

While planning is a process onto itself, the planning process should serve to provide a firm foundation upon which to build other aspects of the management system. In the case of the ILO guidelines, the purpose of the planning process should be to create an OSH management system that supports compliance with local or national laws and regulations, the elements of the organization's OSH management system, and continual improvement in OSH performance.

The fundamental objective of a planning process is to set very clear mandates and expectations for the management system. The occupational safety and health management system in the organization should ensure:

- a clear definition, priority setting, and quantification, where appropriate, of the organization's OSH objectives

- the preparation of a plan for achieving each objective, with defined responsibility and clear performance criteria indicating what is to be done, by whom, and when

- the selection of measurement criteria for confirming that the objectives are achieved

- the provision of adequate resources, including human and financial resources and technical support, as appropriate

Occupational Safety and Health Objectives

One of the most important features of any management system is whether there are clear, reasonable, and value-added objectives by which the business will be both judged and measured. This can be a challenge, especially when the SMART acronym is not used as an objective-setting guideline. More and more organizations are moving to a balanced scorecard approach to measure the effectiveness of their management system and processes. In the occupational health and safety arena, the concept of leading and lagging indicators is becoming a common industry phrase. Yet while identifying lagging safety indicators is typically something many safety practitioners feel comfortable with, determining value-added leading safety management system indicators has posed a challenge to some in the safety profession.

Section 3.9.1 of the ILO guidelines suggests that consistent with the OSH policy and based on the initial or subsequent reviews, measurable OSH objectives should be established, which are:

- specific to the organization and appropriate to and according to its size and nature of activity

- consistent with the relevant and applicable local or national laws and regulations and the technical and business obligations of the organization with regard to OSH

- focused toward continually improving workers' OSH protection to achieve the best OSH performance

- realistic and achievable

- documented and communicated to all relevant functions and levels of the organization

- periodically evaluated and, if necessary, updated

Hazard Prevention

Inherent in the approach to safety management is the expectation that hazards and risks to workers' safety and health should be identified and assessed on an ongoing basis.

Similar to the hierarchy of controls referenced in Section 5.1.1 of Z10, the ILO guideline offers a similar hierarchy to help rationalize a systematic approach to risk management. This hierarchy provides a very reasonable method to help define a systematic way to determine the method by which risk is identified, assessed, and managed. In fact, this suggested hierarchy is deemed by some to be at the very heart of any successful safety management system.

The ILO management system guidelines suggest preventive and protective measures should be implemented in the following order of priority, or hierarchy:

- eliminate the hazard/risk

- control the hazard/risk at the source through the use of engineering controls or organizational measures

- minimize the hazard/risk by the design of safe work systems, which include administrative control measures

- provide for appropriate personal protective equipment, including clothing, at no cost, and implement measures to ensure its use and maintenance where residual hazards/risks cannot be controlled by collective measures

The hazard prevention and control procedures established should be adapted to the hazards and risks encountered by the organization, reviewed and modified if necessary on a regular basis, comply with laws and regulations, reflect good practice, and consider the current state of knowledge, including information or reports from organizations such as labor inspectorates, occupational safety and health services, and other services, as appropriate.

Management of change is a management system process that requires a considerable degree of discipline to execute and manage effectively. While deemed by some as being a process that requires too much attention and documentation for the return on investment, management of change for safety management system factors can identify a wide range of critical operational safety issues which, if not managed and communicated well, can lead to critical consequences.

The ILO guidelines require that a workplace hazard identification and risk assessment should be carried out before any modification or introduction of new work methods, materials, processes, or machinery. The guideline requires that these assessments should be carried out in consultation with workers and their representatives and the safety and health committee, where appropriate.

Emergency Prevention, Preparedness, and Response Even in the most prudent and diligent of organizations, sometimes things can, and do, go wrong. And while there may be factors that are not always within the direct control of the organization, as the Boy Scout motto says, "always be prepared." Emergency response protocols and response plans can demonstrate due diligence in those instances where the plans and programs, for whatever reason, fail to achieve their stated or intended objectives.

The ILO guidelines require that emergency prevention, preparedness, and response arrangements should be established and maintained and they should identify the potential for accidents and emergency situations and address the prevention of OSH risks associated with them.

Like any rationalized approach to a safety management system, the ILO guidelines require that the arrangements should be made according to the size, nature, and scope of activity of the organization. They should also:

- ensure that the necessary information, internal communication, and coordination are provided to protect all people in the event of an emergency at the work site

- provide information to, and communication with, the relevant competent authorities and the neighborhood and emergency response services

- address first aid and medical assistance, firefighting, and emergency evacuation of all people at the work site

- provide relevant information and training to all members of the organization, at all levels, including regular exercises in emergency prevention, preparedness, and response procedures

There is also an expectation that emergency prevention, preparedness, and response arrangements should be established in cooperation with external emergency services and other bodies where applicable. These typically can include fire and police, hospitals, emergency response organizations, government agencies, and nongovernmental agencies or other regulatory bodies.

Procurement Consistent with other standards and their emphasis on purchasing and contractor/supplier management, Section 3.10.4.1. of the ILO guidelines suggest procedures should be established and maintained to ensure that the occupational safety and health management system in the organization is identified, evaluated, and incorporated into purchasing and leasing specifications, local or national laws, and regulations. The organizations that own OSH requirements should be identified prior to the procurement of goods and services, and arrangements should be made to achieve conformance to the requirements prior to their use.

For contract services, the guidelines suggest arrangements should be established and maintained for ensuring that the organization's safety and health requirements, or at least the equivalent, are applied to contractors and their workers. The arrangements for contractors working on-site should include OSH criteria in procedures for evaluating and selecting contractors and establishing effective ongoing communication and coordination between appropriate levels of the organization and the contractor prior to commencing work. This should include provisions for communicating hazards and the measures to prevent and control them and arrangements for the reporting of work-related injuries, ill health, diseases, and incidents among the contractors' workers while performing work for them.

Organization, provision for relevant workplace safety and health hazard awareness, and training to contractors or their workers prior to commencing work and as work progresses, as necessary, and regularly monitoring OSH performance of contractor activities on-site and verifying that on-site OSH procedures and arrangements are followed by the contractor(s) are necessary.

Evaluation

Management system auditing has become an entity unto itself, with a wide range of guidance options available to professional management system auditors. While there are many and varied training options available to in-house safety management practitioners with responsibilities for the OHS management system, ILO gives specific guidance on auditing the OHS management system.

Performance Measurement

The ILO guidelines require procedures that have been designed to monitor, measure, and record occupational safety and health performance on a regular basis. In addition to management system establishment, they should also be subject to periodic review consistent with the periodic review requirements of other standards and guidelines for quality and environmental management.

There is also a requirement to establish a framework for responsibility, accountability, and authority to ensure monitoring is carried out at different levels in the management structure.

We reference a wide range of performance indicator options in our chapter on performance measurement. A management system implemented using the ILO guidelines requires the development of appropriate performance indicators based on the size and nature of activity of the organization and the OSH objectives.

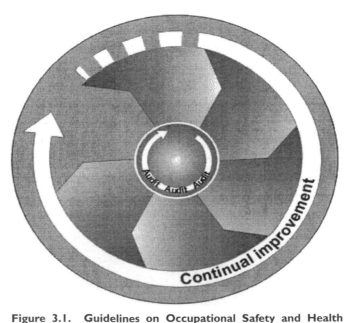

Figure 3.1. Guidelines on Occupational Safety and Health Management Systems ILO-OSH 2001

One of the common themes the authors hear from smaller companies is that the size and scope of a structured management system, based on ISO standards or other voluntary guidelines, is just too difficult to manage and requires too many resources. The bottom line is that any rationalized approach to business requires the intelligent dedication of prudent and competent resources to achieve business objectives. The degree to which these systems get designed should be directly proportional to the size, scope, and resources available to that organization to achieve those objectives. This is where the professional experience and integrity of the management system practitioner should play a key role. It would be better to have a management system well-designed, implemented, and executed effectively than to have an ego-driven management system with all the theoretical bells and whistles and no practical way or resources of implementing the system. In other words, don't make a management systems rod to beat your back with.

Performance Monitoring

In order to provide meaningful evaluation of the management system, the ILO guidelines suggest both qualitative and quantitative measures appropriate to the needs of the organization. These measures should be designed based on the organization's identified hazards and risks, the commitments in the OSH policy, and the OSH objectives. They should also support the organization's evaluation process, including the management review.

The ILO guideline for performance monitoring and assessment is expressed in Section 3.11.4. of the guidelines. Performance monitoring and measurement should be used as a means of determining the degree to which the policy and objectives are being implemented as well as the degree to which risks are being controlled. There should also be active and reactive monitoring, and the monitoring should not be based only upon work-related injury, ill health, disease, and incident statistics. Of course, a key part of any management system is documented evidence, and the ILO guidelines suggest recorded evidence of the evaluation process should be captured and maintained.

When it comes to monitoring the management system, the following requirements are suggested by the ILO guidelines:

- feedback on OSH performance

- information to determine whether the day-to-day arrangements for hazard and risk identification, prevention, and control are in place and operating effectively

- the basis for decisions about improvement in hazard identification and risk control and the OSH management system

A key aspect of the active monitoring system should include the elements necessary to have a proactive system. More and more emphasis these days is placed on the before-the-fact measurement of performance—it's a "pay me now or pay me later" scenario. Specific to the requirement of the ILO guidelines, organizations are encouraged to have:

- monitoring of the achievement of specific plans, established performance criteria, and objectives

- systematic inspection of work systems, premises, plant, and equipment

- provisions for the surveillance of the working environment, including work organization

- provisions for the surveillance of workers' health, where appropriate, through suitable medical monitoring or follow-up of workers for early detection of signs and symptoms of harm to health in order to determine the effectiveness of prevention and control measures

- provisions for compliance with applicable national laws and regulations, collective agreements, and other commitments on OSH to which the organization subscribes

Section 3.11.7. of the ILO guidelines suggests that reactive monitoring should include the identification, reporting, and investigation of:

- work-related injuries, ill health (including monitoring of aggregate sickness absence records), diseases, and incidents

- other losses, such as damage to property

- deficient safety and health performance and OSH management system failures

- workers' rehabilitation and health-restoration programs

Investigation and Problem-Solving

The investigation of work-related injuries, ill health, diseases, and incidents and their impact on safety and health performance has been one of the cornerstones of many safety management systems. And while it is typically a reactive exercise, its importance to the analysis of determining where and how the management system may have fallen down is critical to all safety management systems. Many businesses use a wide variety of root cause analysis and problem-solving tools as part of their approach to investigation and problem-solving. A quick search on Google will identify more resources than necessary to effectively help you with this problem-solving process.

The ILO guidelines suggest the investigation of the origin and underlying causes of work-related injuries, ill health, diseases, and incidents should be designed to identify any failures in the OSH management system and that documentation of these findings should be a key aspect of the investigation process. Those who are able to demonstrate competence in the investigation process and techniques should be the ones to conduct accident and incident investigations. Investigations should also include the appropriate participation of workers and their representative, and the results of such investigations should be communicated to the safety and health committee, where it exists, and the committee should make appropriate recommendations.

The results of investigations, in addition to any recommendations from the safety and health committee, should be communicated to appropriate persons internal and external to the organization for corrective action and be included in the management review and consideration for continual improvement activities.

Of course, it is meaningless to conduct an investigation and identify critical improvement opportunities if there is no mechanism or process to ensure the actions stemming from the investigative process get acted upon. The corrective action resulting from such investigations should be implemented in order to avoid repetition of work-related injuries, ill health, diseases, and incidents. The action-tracking system of the organization should be used to manage and track the status of these actions until both their logical and verified conclusion. And as an added issue, the status of open, closed, and late actions can be a key measure of the effectiveness of the management system in action-tracking management. (For more information, see the chapter on IT solutions for your integrated management system.)

Sometimes external agencies are introduced into the investigation process, especially when critical regulations have been breached. The ILO guidelines suggest reports produced by external investigative agencies, such as government inspection agencies or workers' compensation agencies, should be acted upon in the same manner as internal investigations, giving due consideration to the issue of confidentiality. From a due diligence perspective, it is very prudent to ensure timely and effective actions are taken on these external investigation findings and recommendations.

Management System Audit

The requirement to conduct periodic audits of the management system is deemed to be a critical aspect of any management system, and the ILO guidelines are no exception. A key audit objective is to establish whether or not the OSH management system and its elements are in place, adequate, and effective in protecting the safety and health of workers and preventing incidents.

It's suggested that the audit include an evaluation of the organization's OSH management system elements, including:

- OSH policy
- worker participation, responsibility, and accountability
- competence and training
- management system documentation
- communication
- system planning, development, and implementation
- prevention and control measures
- management of change
- emergency prevention, preparedness, and response
- procurement and contracting
- performance monitoring and measurement
- investigation of work-related injuries, ill health, diseases, and incidents and their impact on safety and health performance
- audits
- management review
- preventive and corrective action
- continual improvement and any other audit criteria or elements that may be appropriate based on the business and regulatory realities of the business

The independence of auditors is a requirement of the guideline, although it should be acknowledged that in many organizations, the policies and procedures associated with the safety, environmental, and quality management system consists of those typically put together by the staff management system professional or quality or safety practitioner. The audit results and audit conclusions should be communicated to those who have responsibility for corrective action and should be considered for inclusion in the annual management review.

Management Review

The management review requirement of Section 3.14.1. of the ILO guidelines requires management to evaluate the overall strategy of the OSH management system to determine whether it meets planned performance objectives. It also requires management to evaluate the OSH management system's ability to meet the overall needs of the organization and its stakeholders, including its workers and the regulatory authorities, and to evaluate the need for changes to the OSH management system, including OSH policy and objectives; identifying what action is necessary to remedy any deficiencies in a timely manner (including adaptations of other aspects of the organization's management structure and performance measurement); providing the feedback direction, including the determination of priorities for meaningful planning and continual improvement; evaluating progress toward the organization's OSH objectives and corrective action activities; and evaluating the effectiveness of follow-up actions from earlier management reviews.

The management review should consider aspects and initiatives deemed critical to the effectiveness of the management system, including the results of work-related injuries, ill health, diseases, and incident investigations; performance monitoring and measurement; and audit activities; and any additional internal and external inputs as well as changes, including organizational changes, that could affect the OSH management system.

Preventive and Corrective Action

It's been generally acknowledged that no system is inherently perfect, especially when subject to the inconsistencies people can bring to the process based on their individual characteristics, biases, and personal focus. The ILO guidelines require a process be established and maintained for preventive and corrective action resulting from OSH management system performance monitoring and measurement, OSH management system audits, and management reviews.

The expectations of the action-tracking process have been designed to ensure the identification and analysis of root causes of any nonconformity with safety regulations, planning, implementation, and checking the effectiveness of corrective and preventive action, including changes to the OSH management system.

Improvement

Continual improvement is a feature of the ILO safety management system, consistent with other management system standards. With respect to continual improvement, section 3.16.1 of the ILO guidelines note that arrangement should be established and maintained for the continual improvement of the relevant elements of the OSH management system. Typical areas of focus include

OSH objectives; results of hazard and risk identifications and assessments; results of performance monitoring and measurements; investigation of work-related injuries, diseases, ill health, and incidents; the results and recommendations of audits; outcomes of the management review; recommendations for improvement from all members of the organization (including the safety and health committee, where it exists); changes in national laws and regulations; voluntary programs and collective agreements; new relevant information; and the results of health protection and promotion programs.[4]

ANSI Z10: A Blueprint for Health and Safety Management Systems in the United States

In North America there are now two different management system standards for health and safety management systems for both the Canadian and American side of the border. In 2005, the United States introduced their version of an occupational health and safety management system known as ANSI/AIHA Z10-2005. The American National Standards Institute (ANSI)/American Industrial Hygiene Association (AIHA) Z10-2005 Occupational Safety and Health Management Systems encourages users and businesses to reduce the risks of injuries, illnesses, and fatalities in a cost-effective manner through the practical implementation of the Z10 requirements.

Quality, environmental, and occupational health and safety (QHSE) management systems are used by many organizations in the United States and around the world. Many of the more commonly known quality and environmental management systems are frequently in conformance to international voluntary consensus standards (i.e., ISO 9001:2000, ISO 14001:2004, etc.), or they share many of the same basic concepts and principles with them. The development of national OH&S management system standards, such as those published by both Canada and the United States, is a more recent phenomenon. But it speaks clearly to the value and importance these two countries place on the benefit of a structured approach to management system requirements for effective safety and health management, regardless of which side of the border in North America. Like the saying goes, if millions of people see the value, there must be something to it.

Home Grown and Custom Built

Many organizations operate their own occupational health and safety management systems (OHSMS) that they have developed using in-house resources and expertise, while others use management systems that conform to commercially available guidelines. Until the development of the ANSI Z10 voluntary consensus standard, there was no U.S. OHSMS consensus standard. Similarly, in Canada, until the development of the CSA Z1000-06 Occupational Health and Safety Management Standard, there was no uniquely Canadian standard for safety management systems. Within the management system community there is widespread agreement that the use of management systems can improve organizational performance, including performance in the occupational health and safety arena. There's just continued debate about which approach works best.

In the United States, the Occupational Safety and Health Administration's (OSHA) Voluntary Protection Program (VPP) relies on management system principles and has reported success in improving occupational health and safety performance among participating companies. In addition, the American Chemistry Council (ACC) reports success in improving the environmental performance of participating organizations. But until Z10, there was no generally accepted, consensus-based standard for occupational health and safety management.

The basic elements of the Z10 standard address such areas as management leadership and employee participation, planning, implementation, evaluation, audit, corrective action, and management review. As is evident when looking at the U.S. safety management system standard, in many important aspects, Z10 encompasses many of the basic tenets that the Occupational Safety and Health Administration (OSHA) first advocated in its draft safety and health management standard, which was later withdrawn from its regulatory agenda.[5]

However, the Z10 standard goes beyond the OSHA draft standard's requirements because it also contains provisions that address risk controls, audits, incident/accident investigations, responsibilities, and authorities. In looking at the relationship of the Z10 to other standards and guidelines, such as Z1000, OHSAS 18001:2007, and the ILO guidelines, it is clear that these provisions are deemed essential in the management of an effective safety system.

It has been suggested that it is unlikely that OSHA will resume regulatory activity concerning its withdrawn safety and health management standard under the current administration. However, if it should proceed in the future, it would be statutorily required to consider adoption of ANSI Z10 to address this issue based upon the requisites of the National Technology Transfer and Advancement Act (NTTAA), 15 USC §272, and the Office of Management and Budget's (OMB) Circular A-119, *Federal Participation in the Development and Use of Voluntary Consensus Standards and in Conformity Assessment Activities*. The OMB circular (consistent with Section 12[d] of the NTTAA) directs agencies to use voluntary consensus standards in lieu of developing government-unique standards, except when such use would be inconsistent with the law or otherwise impractical.

However, under the current OSH Act, only national consensus standards that have been adopted as or incorporated by reference into an OSHA standard pursuant to Section 6 of the OSH Act provide a means of compliance with Section 5(a)(2) of the Occupational Safety and Health Act, 29 U.S.C. §651 et seq. ("the OSH Act").[6] Therefore, at some future time, OSHA could adopt Z10 as a mandatory safety and health standard through notice-and-comment rulemaking.

The major professional health and safety organizations are also on record in support of management systems as effective tools for improving health and safety performance, as well as for contributing to the overall success of the business.

Finally, the fact that many organizations in the United States and abroad are implementing management systems in occupational health and safety is evidence that these systems add value to their businesses and to the economy. The good news for management system practitioners in the United States and Canada is that both Z10 and Z1000, while deemed voluntary consensus standards, were developed with the input and agreement of business, labor, and government and received significant input from committees representing the broadly based interests of these groups, in addition to professional organizations and general interest groups.

A Brief History of ANSI/AIHA Z10

In 1999, the American National Standards Institute officially approved the ANSI Accredited Standards Committee Z10, with the American Industrial Hygiene Association as its secretariat, to begin work on a U.S. OH&S standard. A committee was formed with broad representation from industry, labor, government, professional organizations, and general interest participants. The committee examined then current national and international standards, guidelines, and practices in the occupational, environmental, and quality systems areas.

Based on extensive discussion, research, and deliberations, they adapted the common principles most relevant from these approaches into a standard that is compatible with the principal international standards as well as with management system approaches currently in use in the United States. The process of developing and issuing a national consensus standard was expected to encourage the use of management system principles and guidelines for occupational health and safety among American organizations. It was also felt that effective implementation would provide widespread benefits in health and safety as well as in productivity, financial performance, and quality and other business goals.

ANSI Z10 is a voluntary consensus standard on occupational health and safety management systems. Like the Canadian Z10, the value placed on the word *consensus* should not be marginalized or underestimated. It uses recognized management system principles in order to be compatible with quality and environmental management system standards such as the ISO 9001:2000 QMS and ISO

14000 EMS. The ANSI Z10 standard also draws very deliberately from approaches used by the International Labor Organization's (ILO) guidelines on occupational health and safety management systems and from systems in use in organizations in the United States. This compatibility encourages integration of the ANSI Z10 standard requirements into other business management systems (ISO 9001:2000 and ISO 14000) in order to enhance overall organizational performance. In Canada, the ILO guidelines on occupational health and safety management systems also formed a significant part of the discussion and focus of the development of Canada's Z1000. Indeed, Z10 also figured very prominently in Canadian discussions about the drafting of Z1000.

Each organization electing to conform to the ANSI Z10 standard is expected to rationalize and determine how it will evaluate its conformance to the standard. The purpose of the standard is to provide organizations with an effective tool for continual improvement of their occupational health and safety performance. A management system implemented in conformance with the ANSI Z10 standard is intended to help organizations minimize workplace risks and reduce the occurrence and cost of occupational injuries, illnesses, and fatalities. The key thing to keep in mind is that while many aspects of how organizations manage workplace health and safety are similar, many aspects are also very different. The Z10 standard is designed to give flexibility, creativity, and risk-based options for an organization to develop and customize their safety management system to meet their current business and regulatory realities.

Many organizations may have already developed an existing occupational health and safety management system appropriate to their needs that may not conform precisely to the ANSI Z10 standard. In those instances, the standard may serve as a voluntary tool to identify possible opportunities to improve their systems by conducting a gap analysis against the requirement of Z10, comparing those gaps with their existing OH&SMS, and developing a strategy to close, address, or rationalize those gaps.

The ANSI Z10 OH&S Management System Approach

The occupational health and safety management system cycle entails an initial planning process and implementation of the management system, followed by a process for checking the management system performance and taking appropriate corrective actions based on the findings of the assessment.

The next step, consistent with other management system standards, requires a management review of the system for suitability, adequacy, and effectiveness against the organization's stated OH&S policy and the requirements of the Z10 standard.

The whole process is then repeated, resulting in (hopefully) ongoing continual improvements in occupational health and safety. Improvement results from reducing hazards and risks in a systematic manner. This is a goal that has been traditionally pursued through independent safety programs that often are not coordinated through a set of common management principles and processes.

In addition to the direct benefits of improved employee health and safety, an OHS management system can also yield positive business outcomes, including enhanced productivity, financial performance, and employee satisfaction.

The management system approach is characterized by its emphasis on continual improvement and systematically eliminating the underlying or root causes of health and safety deficiencies that may cause injuries or even death of an employee. For example, in a systems approach, if an inspection finds an unguarded machine, not only would the unguarded machine be fixed but there would also be a systematic process in place to discover and eliminate the underlying reason for the deficiency.

This process might then lead to the goal of replacing the guards with a more effective design or to replacement of the machines themselves so that the hazard is eliminated. This systematic approach seeks a long-term solution rather than a one-time fix.

The ANSI Z10 OH&S Management System Format

The ANSI Z10 standard is formatted into two columns to help distinguish requirements from recommended practices and explanatory information. Requirements are in the left column and are identified by the word "shall." An organization that chooses to conform to the ANSI Z10 standard is expected to fulfill these requirements. The text in the right-hand column uses the word "should" to describe recommended or best practices, or explanatory notes to the requirements on the left. This use of the terms "shall" and "should" to identify requirements and distinguish them from recommendations and explanatory notes is common practice in ANSI and other international standards.

ANSI Z10 Approval Process

The ANSI Z10 standard was processed and approved through ANSI by the Z10 Accredited Standards Committee on Occupational Health and Safety Management Systems. Many organizations that choose to go down the path of an implemented formal management system seek external verification and registration of that management system, although some choose, for various reasons, not to have an independent third party audit their management system.

ANSI Z10 Certification Requirements Process

A common process for organizations seeking to have their management system recognized/certified to the requirements of Z10 is typically based around the following structure:

Stage 1: On-Site Audit Preparation and Documentation Review

Approximately two to four weeks in advance of the certification audit activity, the registrar will schedule an on-site Stage 1 assessment of the ANSI Z10 management system documentation, including your quality manual and procedures. The documentation will be reviewed during the course of the on-site Stage 1 assessment to determine that the documentation adequately addresses the requirements of ANSI Z10.

Additionally the Stage 1 assessment will provide for a review of the organizations resources, scope of the OH&S management system, related statutory and regulatory aspects and requirements, and OH&S processes. This assessment will give the assessor the opportunity to gain an understanding of the organization in preparation for the Stage 2 audit.

The Stage 1 assessment will provide a focus for planning the Stage 2 assessment so that the assessor can gain sufficient understanding of the organizations ANSI Z10 OH&S management system and site operations in preparation for the Stage 2 Initial Certification Audit. An audit schedule will also be drafted during the Stage 1 assessment.

Any significant omissions identified by the registrar will be reported in writing. During Stage 1, the audit checklist will be developed to enable the audit team to reference applicable requirements within the organization's documented system prior to conducting the Stage 2 initial audit.

Stage 2: On-Site Final Certification Audit Activity

The Stage 2 initial audit typically consists of an on-site evaluation of the implemented OH&S management system as well as the ANSI Z10 requirements. In reviewing the adequacy and effectiveness of your OH&S management system, the auditors will generally interview personnel in any department or area who have responsibilities and authorities associated with the intended scope of the registration.

Audit results are reported verbally at the conclusion of the audit and subsequently in a written report. Any major system weakness or nonconformance to the standard identified during the initial audit must be addressed to the satisfaction of the registrar prior to the registration of the OH&S management system.

The ANSI Z10 Registration/Certification Decision Process

Following the on-site Stage 1 and Stage 2 initial audit activities, members of the registrar's certification committee will review the audit team's recommendation, written report, and all associated documentation independently. When this review determines that all requirements have been met, STR-R will certify and register the organization and issue the ANAB Accredited ANSI Z10 (OHSAS) Certificate of Conformance to the organization.

This certificate is valid for three years. Upon receipt of the ANSI Z10 registration certificate, registered clients are entitled to use the STR-R Certification Mark and ANAB Mark to advertise their achievement. In the case of STR-R, the STR-R Certification Mark is permitted.

Surveillance Audits

Surveillance audits are conducted annually after the date of the conclusion of the initial certification audit and may be held in conjunction with other surveillance audit activity. These audits are conducted to determine that the OH&S management system continues to be implemented in accordance with planned arrangements stated in your management system and that the system continues to be compliant to the requirements of the ANSI Z10 standard.

Surveillance audits may be performed at six-, nine-, or twelve-month increments at the organization's discretion, but they must total the number of audit days per year cited in our summary of audit time.

Third-Year Recertification

Recertification audits are conducted every third year following the initial certification audit to verify that the organization continues to satisfy the ANSI Z10 standard requirements under which they've been registered. ANSI Z10 recertification audits may be held in conjunction with the organization's ISO 9001:2000 QMS or AS9100 AQMS recertification audit activity.

As opposed to annual surveillance audits, the recertification audit is more in-depth and closely resembles the initial certification audit, though of slightly reduced duration. Audit results are reported verbally at the conclusion of the audit and subsequently in a written report. Any major nonconformance to the standard identified must be corrected to the satisfaction of the registrar, prior to recommendation to the certification committee for renewed registration of your system.

Upon conclusion of the audit, the registrar's certification committee will review the audit team's recommendation, written report, and all associated documentation independently to verify that all requirements have been met. Once satisfied, the registrar will recertify the organization and reissue a new ANSI Z10

Certificate of Conformance to the organization for the scope of the services evaluated. This new certificate shall be valid for three years, subject to continued conformance through surveillance. In rare cases, a Stage 1 audit may be necessary.

The Client's Prerequisite Requirements

The registration process requires that an operational OH&S management system be in place at the time of the audit. This means that at a minimum:

- The OH&S system is fully documented and has been implemented.

- The OH&S internal audit system is fully implemented, with one complete round of internal OH&S audits completed and the OH&S management system demonstrates effectiveness.

- A complete OH&S management review cycle has been carried out.

- A management representative has been appointed who is responsible for ensuring complete implementation of the OH&S management system and who will assist the audit team during the assessment process.[7]

The information above was reproduced with the permission of Bryce E. Carson Sr., president & CEO and STR Registrar LLC (STR-R). STR-Registrar LLC (STR-R) is an ANSI/ASQ National Accreditation Board (ANAB) and an international provider of management system registrations to the ISO 9001:2000, AS9100, and the ANSI/AIHA Z10: 2005 standards. STR Registrar, LLC also certifies organizations to the British standard, OHSAS 18001:2007. They can be reached at the following website, www.str-r.com/, or by calling toll free 800-903-5660.

The registration process is a diligent process, but it is one that can help ensure a strong, value-added QHSE management system for the benefit of all stakeholders.

CSA Z1000-06: The New Canadian Standard for OHS Management

While theoretical references and discussions about management systems are always relevant, even more relevant is the practical application of a management system to the real world. In June 2006, I wrote an article for SafetyXChange.com informing North American readers, and especially Canadians, about the publication of a groundbreaking safety standard recently introduced in Canada.

The first-ever Canadian consensus-based standard was issued by the Canadian Standards Association (CSA) in March 2006. Entitled CSA Z1000-06 Occupational Health and Safety Management, the standard provides a model for developing and implementing an occupational health and safety management system (OHSMS). In a nutshell, here's a capsule summary of its application for the Canadian workplace.

Safety, But With a Business Purpose

The stated purpose of CSA Z1000-06 is to enable an organization to advance its occupational health and safety performance by establishing, maintaining, and/or improving an occupational health and safety management system. By doing so, the organization should be better able to identify, eliminate, or control hazards and risks while ensuring conformity with their occupational health and safety policy. But Z1000-06 was crafted for another reason. In addition to significant safety and health benefits, the intent of the standard is to help organizations achieve other business goals, including improvement in productivity, financial performance, and quality.

How the Standard Works . . . A Management System Journey

Like many other management systems, the Z1000 standard is structured in accordance with the Plan-Do-Check-Act (PDCA) approach common to other management system standards, such as ISO 9001:2000 or ISO 14001:2004. The PDCA approach provides a logical framework for managing preventive and protective measures, emergency preparedness, training, procurement issues, documentation, legal, and other safety-related requirements.

The intent is for the occupational health and safety management system to incorporate all standard requirements. But the extent of the application will depend on the circumstances particular to each organization, such as the nature and location of its operations and the conditions under which it functions, including regulatory realities. In other words, Z1000 is a performance-based standard.

According to CSA, implementing the standard encourages "a more systematic approach to meeting defined OHS objectives and helps increase awareness of health and safety in the workplace."[8] It also motivates Canadian organizations to implement an occupational health and safety management system that meets the requirements of a recognized standard and forms a framework through which other Canadian OHS standards can be applied.

A Uniquely Canadian Flavor

Canadian OHS laws are based to a large degree on the principles known as the Internal Responsibility System (IRS) in which workplace stakeholders, including management and workers, work together to achieve their own health and safety goals and objectives. CSA Z-1000-06 is steeped in the IRS tradition. Specifically, it stresses the need for worker participation in the operation of the management system, ensuring that all parties contribute to the organization's success.

Organizations can demonstrate adherence to the standard by making a self-determination and self-declaration. Organizations can self-declare their conformance to the CSA Z-1000 standard through their own resources, through an outside party (independent of the organization), or by gaining certification/registration of its occupational health and safety management system by a management systems registrar, similar to other management system options.

Potential Impact for the Great White North

The CSA Z1000-06 represents an important step in the evolution of the practice of safety in Canada. Realistically, some have suggested that over time it might become the Canadian benchmark against which safety and health management systems will be measured. This is not to say that other safety management systems have considerable value, or that eventually there may be an ISO standard for health and safety management systems that will become an international standard; however, one of the strengths of Z1000 (in addition to Z10) is that it is a consensus-based standard. And the authors can vouch for the fact that labor, management, government, and other interest groups had a fair and equitable say in the development of the standard. From a marketing perspective, Z1000 holds great potential as a best-practice, due-diligence standard for Canadian workplaces. On another positive note, even if ISO does eventually come out with an international standard for OH&S management systems, many of the current expectations in Z1000 will, in the opinion of the authors, be able to be satisfied due in part to the degree of research conducted for Z1000 and many of the similarities of Z1000 to Z10, OHSAS 180001, and the ILO guidelines on occupational health and safety management systems.

Safety, health, and environmental management practitioners should not ignore the long-range impact Z1000-06 will have on societal expectations concerning the quality of safety management systems that employers have in place and on the expectations employers will have concerning the knowledge and capabilities of safety, health, and environmental management personnel. Safety practitioners from Canadian organizations would be prudent to study the requirements of CSA Z1000-06 and determine if they have what it takes to put them into place. If not, they should acquire the necessary skills to do so. The end result will be to further their organization's performance and their own personal career success.[9]

Z1000 ... An Insider's Perspective

Let's start off by clearly stating that the authors hold a special place in their "professional" hearts for Z1000. In addition to it being a standard that impacts the country in which we, for the most part, live and work, one of the coauthors, Terri Andrews, has helped clients understand and implement the standard into their integrated management system, complementing their quality and environmental management systems. As an associate member of the technical committee that researched and wrote the Z1000 standard between 2004 and 2006, coauthor Wayne Pardy was intimately involved in the research and discussion surrounding Z1000. The standard was prepared by the Technical Committee on Occupational Health and Safety Management Systems, under the jurisdiction of the Strategic Steering Committee on Occupational Health and Safety, and was formally approved by the Technical Committee and the Standards Council of Canada as a national standard of Canada.

The authors felt that to give readers a practical perspective on management system standards, a look into the background and current reality of Z1000 would prove beneficial. We will also include some practical advice for management system practitioners with respect to how to consider the wide host of integrated management system options, based on your in-house developed management system or a management system obtained elsewhere.

While there are many variations of in-house and third-party management systems and guidelines, Z1000 was designed to address not only the universal requirements for a modern safety management system but also those unique aspects of the Canadian legislative and safety landscape that make Z1000 particularly useful within a Canadian context for an integrated management system. A quick scan of the contents of Z1000 and the reader will quickly see that similarities with OHSAS 18001, Z10, and the ILO guidelines on occupational health and safety management systems are evident. For those looking to develop a management system, one of the first and more obvious places to start is in the arena of management systems currently in use, or research about them. So it's no small coincidence that in looking at the design and structure of Z1000, similarities with the above-noted standards and guidelines as well as ISO 14001:2004 and ISO 9001:2000 exist. The following are the general section headings under which the scope of Z1000 bases its expectations:

Z1000 Scope

Occupational Health and Safety Management System
General
Commitment, Leadership, and Participation
    General
    Management Commitment and Leadership
    Worker Participation
    Occupational Health and Safety Policy

Planning
> **General**
> **Review**
> **Legal and Other Requirements**
> **Hazard and Risk Identification and Assessment**
> **Occupational Health and Safety Objectives and Targets**

Implementation
> **General**
> **Preventive and Protective Measures**
> **Emergency Prevention, Preparedness, and Response**
> **Competence and Training**
> **Communication and Awareness**
> **Procurement and Contracting**
> **Management of Change**
> **Documentation**

Evaluation and Corrective Action
> **General**
> **Monitoring and Measurement**
> **Incident Investigation and Analysis**
> **Internal Audits**
> **Preventive and Corrective Action**

Management Review and Continual Improvement

General

Continual improvement

Review Input

Review output

Z1000 specifies the requirements for an occupational health and safety management system (OHSMS) within the Canadian context of the respective legislative jurisdictions in which the Z1000 is applicable—namely Canada and its respective provinces. In the preamble, CSA notes that the purpose of the standard is to enable an organization to improve its occupational health and safety (OHS) performance and thus reduce or prevent occupational injuries, illnesses, and fatalities, by:

- establishing, maintaining, and improving an OHSMS that will identify and then eliminate or control all OHS hazards and risks

- ensuring conformity with its OHS policy

- demonstrating conformity with this standard by making a self-determination and self-declaration, receiving confirmation of its self-declaration by an outside party, independent of the organization or gaining certification/registration of its OHSMS by an outside organization

The requirements of the standard have been designed to be incorporated into any occupational health and safety management system. The extent of the application will depend on the circumstances particular to the organization, such as the nature and location of its operations and the conditions in which it functions. The standard specifies all the appropriate requirements for an occupational health and safety management system (OHSMS), and Z1000 is deemed to be applicable to an organization of any size or type and is intended to address occupational health and safety and not product and services safety.

A positive aspect of Z1000 is the inclusion of an annex that provides guidance on the practical use, application, and interpretation of the standard. While the annex is not a mandatory part of the standard, it is a welcome and useful addition to any management system practitioner, as there are always questions to be asked in the interpretation and meaning of any standard and the availability of the guidance on the use of CSA Z1000-06 is certainly a positive aspect of the standard.[10] The guidance is also very useful during the management system audit process.

Which Standard Is Best?

The authors are often asked which standard to use if a company is interested in seeking to structure and implement a formal management system. It's been our experience that Canadians ask questions about Z1000. Americans ask about Z10. Those with international operations ask about a standard 18001:2007 or the ILO management system guidelines. Our advice to any and all that have asked is this: For those with operations unique to a single country, give serious consideration to the standard of the country in which you live. As some of the requirements of Z10 and Z1000 reflect some of the unique characteristics of the regulatory environment in which those standards have been developed, it is prudent to consider their practical application for your environment. If you have operations that are international in scope, it might be beneficial to consider a management system standard that may be able to be universally applied, regardless of the regulatory environment in which it is being used. This is not meant to lessen the value of any standard or guidelines. It is simply advice given that a prudent management system practitioner should consider, based on the organizational, legal, and other regulatory realities of his or her business.[11]

Comparative Analysis of Management Systems and Guidelines

For those looking for additional guidance and suggestions for conducting a comparative approach to some of the various management systems, practices, and guidelines, the Department of Defense Office of the Inspector General, in cooperation with the National Safety Council, has produced a comparative analysis of safety and health management systems. Their comparative analysis (CA) model identifies a number of common elements that are noted to be characteristic of some of the more notable, effective safety management systems and culture-maturity models identified during their study.

It's been suggested that organizations should consider the use of tools such as the comparative analysis model when designing their safety management systems. The National Safety Council's website notes,

> Careful examination of these elements can be beneficial to organizations and decision makers when establishing a new or re-engineering an existing enterprise-wide safety and health program. The CA suggests that each system is built on an organizational safety philosophy that promotes a structured approach with measurable attributes and milestones. This analysis validates the notion that creating and sustaining an effective organizational safety culture requires a deliberate architecture based on four elements:
>
> - Leadership
> - Management
> - Employee relations
> - Measurement
>
> Best practice has been promoted as a leading strategic element in the development of modern management system because, according to the National Safety Council, high performing organizations promote safety and adopt safety as one of their core values. Since employees expect to work in an environment that is safe and healthy, leaders and managers should continually evaluate their safety and health programs to ensure leadership, policies, resources, mechanisms, and tools are achieving the intended outcomes. Mutual trust and accountability among leaders, managers, and employees are inherent in mature safety cultures; therefore, leaders and managers should continually assess the safety climate and culture, and identify improvement opportunities.[12]

Gap Analysis ... A Prudent Management System Due-Diligence Exercise

One of the first places to start in attempting to determine which management system standard meets the requirements and realities of your current organizational reality is to conduct a gap assessment against your current management system structure and the standards you deem will be the best practice model upon which you wish to build your new management system. There are several ways in which this can be accomplished. One of the ways is simply to obtain a copy of a standard and "match" the aspects of the standard in question against the current practices of your in-house developed management system structure. In addition to a gap analysis, conducting a baseline audit against the requirements of the management system standard is also a prudent step. While the baseline audit will take more time and involve documenting more objective evidence than the gap analysis, it is still a valuable exercise. By way of further example, if you would like to see how your current management system stacks up against the requirements of Z1000, use the following baseline audit, based on the requirement of Z1000, to see where you match up or where your gaps may be. This practical exercise will give you a good feel of how much or how little work you may have to do to bring your organization up to the requirements of Z1000.

Z1000 Baseline Audit ... How Does Your Management System Stack Up?

Ask these questions of your current management system and see where you stand and how you compare:

1. Is senior management commitment evident in:
   - establishing, promoting, and maintaining the organization's OHSMS?
   - the provision of appropriate financial, human, and organizational resources for planning, implementing, checking, reviewing, and correcting the OHSMS?
   - defining roles, assigning responsibilities, establishing accountability, and delegating authority to implement the OHSMS?
   - establishing and implementing an OHS policy and measurable objectives?
   - ensuring that workers and worker representatives are consulted?
   - providing for active participation by workers and worker representatives in the establishment and maintenance of the OHSMS?

2. Has senior management appointed someone who, irrespective of other duties, has the responsibility and authority to:
   - ensure that the OHSMS is established, maintained, and reviewed?
   - report to senior management on the performance of the OHSMS and any need for improvement?
   - support the participation of the workplace parties?

3. Are workers and worker representatives given the time and resources to participate effectively in the OHSMS?

4. Are there mechanisms provided to support worker participation?

5. Are worker and worker representatives trained in, and consulted on, all aspects of OHS associated with their work?

6. If worker recommendations are not accepted, are reasons provided for not acting on them?

7. Does your OHS policy demonstrate management's commitment to protect workers and continually improve OHS performance?

8. Is your policy periodically reviewed and updated?

9. Does your review process gather and assess information related to:
   - existing OHS processes and programs?
   - previous OHS assessments?
   - processes for communication and awareness?
   - processes for procurement and contracting?
   - processes for incident investigation?
   - processes for OHS training and educational activities?
   - human, financial, and technical resources assigned to OHS processes and programs?
   - other relevant management systems in use and other related activities?

10. Has the organization established and maintained a procedure to identify and access applicable legal and other requirements?

11. Do you keep track of changes to legal and other requirements?

12. Do you periodically evaluate compliance with legal and other requirements?

13. Does your organization incorporate these legal and other requirements in the OHSMS as necessary?

14. Has your organization established and maintained a process to identify and assess hazards and risks on an ongoing basis?

15. Does your process take into account:
   - workplace inspections?
   - workplace health and safety committee recommendations?
   - workers' or worker representatives' concerns or complaints?

- investigations of incidents or near misses?
- worker illness or injury records?
- legal and other requirements?
- material safety data sheets?
- equipment manufacturer's specifications/instructions?
- related hazard alerts or bulletins?

16. Are the results of this process used to set objectives and targets?

17. Are OHS objectives and targets consistent with the organization's policy and based on its review?

18. Have workers and worker representatives participated in the development of the objectives and targets?

19. Has a plan to meet the organization's objectives and targets been developed?

20. Does your plan include the designation of responsibility and means and the time frame for the achievement of the objectives and targets?

21. Are your objectives and targets regularly reviewed to ensure that they continue to reflect desired improvements in OHS performance?

22. Are your objectives and targets measurable?

23. Have adequate resources been assigned to achieve conformity with the standard?

24. Does your organization include, or have access to, people with the competence to implement the standard?

25. Does your organization develop preventive and protective measures according to the hierarchy specified in the Z1000 standard?

26. Has your organization established and maintained emergency prevention, preparedness, and response procedures that:
    - identify potential emergency situations?
    - define the responses to emergency situations?
    - identify the necessary resources?
    - require periodic testing of emergency plans?
    - specify review and update procedures?
    - are communicated to workers?
    - specify necessary training?
    - are communicated to contractors, visitors, and relevant emergency response services?

27. Has your organization established and maintained a procedure to:
    - define the competence requirements for workers?
    - ensure that workers are competent to carry out all OHS aspects of their duties and responsibilities?
    - ensure that workers are aware of applicable OHSMS requirements and their OHS rights and responsibilities?
    - communicate the importance of compliance with the OHS policy, procedural rules, and legal and other requirements?
    - ensure that workers are aware of the potential consequences of noncompliance?

28. Are training activities:
    - provided to all workers, based on their duties and responsibilities?
    - conducted by competent persons?
    - delivered effectively and in a timely manner?
    - evaluated by participants in the training activity?
    - modified as necessary to ensure relevance and effectiveness?
    - documented appropriately?

29. Has your organization established and maintained procedures to:
    - communicate information about the OHSMS?
    - communicate information about the OHS policy and the progress of the implementation plan?
    - receive, document, and respond to internal and external OHS communications?
    - report workplace injuries, illnesses, incidents, hazards, and risks?
    - receive, consider, and respond to the OHS concerns, ideas, and inputs of workers and worker representatives in a timely fashion?
    - consult with workplace health and safety committees or worker representatives?

30. Has your organization established a process to evaluate products, supplies, equipment, raw materials, and other goods to:
    - identify and assess the associated hazards and risks?
    - eliminate or control these hazards and risks?
    - ensure that these goods conform to OHS requirements?

31. Has your organization established and maintained procedures to:
    - evaluate and select contractors?
    - identify, assess, and eliminate or control hazards and risks to the organization's workers arising from the contractor's activities and materials on the organization's premises?

- identify, assess, and eliminate or control hazards and risks to contractors and their workers arising from the organization's activities and materials?

32. Has your organization established and maintained procedures to identify:
    - the hazards and risks associated with new processes or operations at the design stage?
    - significant changes to its work procedures, equipment, organizational structures, staffing, products, services, or suppliers?
    - developments in OHS knowledge and technology?
    - changes to OHS legislation, collective agreements, or other requirements?

33. Are hazard and risk identifications and assessments carried out before any modification or introduction of work methods, materials, processes, machinery, or equipment in the workplace?

34. Are assessments performed by a competent person?

35. Is there appropriate participation by workers and worker representatives?

36. Has your organization created and maintained the documents and records:
    - specified by its OHSMS?
    - required to implement the OHSMS effectively?
    - required to assess conformance with the requirements of this standard?

37. Is documentation clearly written and easily understood?

38. Does your OHSMS documentation include:
    - the organization's OHS policy and performance measures?
    - the assignment of duties and responsibilities for the implementation of the OHSMS?
    - the procedures required by this standard?
    - supporting documents that ensure the effective planning, implementation, operation, and control of its OHSMS?
    - other documents and records required by the standard, including those to show compliance with legal requirements?

39. Are the documents required by the OHSMS controlled?

40. Has your organization established a documented procedure for the control of documents?

41. Does your documented procedure define the controls needed to:
    - approve documents for adequacy before use?
    - review, update, or withdraw documents?
    - ensure that changes to the document and the current revision of the document are identified?
    - ensure that relevant versions of applicable documents are available at points of use?
    - ensure that documents remain legible and readily identifiable?
    - ensure that documents of an external origin are identified and their distribution controlled?
    - prevent the unintended use of obsolete documents and identify such documents if they are retained for any purpose?

42. Has your organization established a documented procedure to control OHS records?

43. Are OHS records legible, readily identifiable, and retrievable?

44. Does your documented procedure specify the controls needed for the identification, storage, protection, retrieval, retention, and disposition of records?

45. Has your organization established and maintained procedures to monitor, measure, and record OHS performance and effectiveness on a regular basis?

46. Does your performance monitoring and measurement:
    - determine the extent to which the OHS policy, objectives, and targets are being met?
    - provide feedback on OHS performance?
    - determine whether the day-to-day arrangements for hazard and risk identification, assessment, and elimination or control are in place and operating effectively?
    - provide the basis for decisions regarding the improvement of the OHSMS?

47. Are both qualitative and quantitative measures, appropriate to the needs, size, and nature of the organization, used?

48. Have monitoring and measurement activities been recorded?

49. When monitoring and measurement equipment is used:
    • is it calibrated?
    • is the calibration maintained?
    • are calibration records available?

50. Does your monitoring and measurement include:
    • inspection of work systems, work organization, premises, and equipment?
    • exposure assessment?
    • injury and illness tracking?
    • assessment of worker rehabilitation programs?
    • occupational health assessment?

51. Does your organization have procedures for reporting work-related injuries, illnesses, fatalities, and OHS incidents?

52. Do these procedures include:
    • defined roles and responsibilities?
    • actions to mitigate consequences of these events?
    • implementation and assessment of corrective and preventive actions, as appropriate?

53. Are accident and incident investigations performed by competent persons as soon as possible after the event so that complete and accurate information is obtained?

54. Are the outcomes of investigations documented and communicated to the workplace health and safety committee(s) and to those who are responsible for implementing the corrective action recommendations?

55. Are the outcomes of investigations communicated to external governmental OHS agencies as required?

56. Are accident and incident investigation reports completed by external agencies given to the organization for review and subsequent planning?

57. Has your organization established an audit program?

58. Has your organization conducted audits of the OHSMS at planned intervals?

    Has it been determined that the organization's OHSMS:
    • meets the requirements of this standard Z1000?
    • has been properly implemented and maintained?

59. Are your audit results, conclusions, and corrective action recommendations documented and communicated to those responsible for corrective action?

60. Are workers and worker representatives consulted in the audit process?

61. Has management ensured that corrective actions are taken to eliminate any nonconformance with reference to the OHSMS or this standard identified during the audit?

62. Has your organization established and maintained preventive and corrective action procedures to:
    - address hazards and risks that have not been adequately controlled by the requirements of clause 4.4.2?
    - identify any newly created hazards resulting from preventive and corrective actions?
    - expedite action on inadequately controlled hazards that could cause serious injury and illness?

63. Has your organization considered input from OHSMS performance monitoring and measurement, OHSMS audits, and management reviews when determining corrective and preventive actions?

64. Has your senior management reviewed the organization's OHSMS at planned intervals to ensure its continued suitability, adequacy, and effectiveness?

65. Has your management review assessed opportunities for continual improvement?

66. Does the input to the management review include:
    - results of audits?
    - communications received from workers, worker representatives, and external interested parties?
    - results of investigations of work-related injuries, illnesses, and OHS incidents?
    - information on the status of objectives and targets?
    - information on the status of corrective and preventive actions?
    - follow-up actions from previous management reviews?
    - recommendations for improvement?

67. Does the output of your management review include decisions and actions related to:
    - the need for changes to the organization's OHS policy and objectives?
    - improvements to the effectiveness of the OHSMS and its processes?
    - allocation of resources?

68. Have action plans been developed from the findings of the management review?

69. Are the findings of the management review recorded and provided to the persons responsible for action and to workers and worker representatives?[13]

For Canadian companies and individuals looking for a modern and consensus-based model upon which to base the development and continuous improvement of their occupational health and safety management system, CSA Z1000-06 offers the perfect model. And for those outside Canada, there's nothing wrong with using this standard as a guideline in considering the development of your internal management system.

PERFORMANCE MEASUREMENT: A MANAGEMENT SYSTEM IMPERATIVE

One of the main functions of the staff QHSE professional is to attempt to develop a comprehensive strategy for his or her respective organization. When we say help, this means that the eventual strategy must come as the result of some degree of deliberation and consultation with select stakeholders in the workplace: employer, workers, union, joint OH&S committee, etc. One of the issues that still causes considerable grief and debate for management system practitioners, workers, and management alike is the issue of measuring the effectiveness of the management system and attempting to determine whether all those initiatives are achieving the desired effect: the reduction of both the frequency and severity of work-related incidents and injuries and the risks that can lead to those incidents; the quality of the product or service; or environmental stewardship.

The problem is that while many understand that effective prevention can only come about as a result of a comprehensive management system, many in middle and senior management, and government regulators, for that matter, only want to know about the "bottom line"—the stats. In defense of senior management, the reality is that many of them don't take the time to devote to the various prevention initiatives in as thorough a way as we would hope. Weekly, monthly, or quarterly status reports of how well we are meeting our corporate targets give senior management a chance to "take the pulse" of the management systems. How well are we doing relative to this time last year, or based on the targets that we've set for ourselves this year?

For example, while occupational injury and accident statistics are still a very important part of the safety system, their value, relevance, and role should be clearly understood by all in your business, as the potential for people to overreact exists when these statistics go up in what people feel is an unacceptable level. Conversely, when you have no accident or injury experience data to share, the perception is that everything is being managed well, from a risk perspective, and that safety is "OK."

The following overview represents the most common reasons why accident and injury data should not be used as the "only" safety indicator in your business.

- Most organizations have too few injury accidents to distinguish real trends from random events.

- If more work is done by the same number of people in the same time, increased workload alone may account for an increase in accident or injury rates.

- The length of the absence from work attributed to injury or ill health may be influenced by factors other than the severity of injury or occupational illnesses, such as poor morale, monotonous work, poor management, opinions of doctors, the age of the worker.

- Accidents may often be underreported (and occasionally over-reported). Levels of reporting can change. They may improve as a result of increased workforce awareness and better reporting and recording systems.

- A time delay may occur between safety system failures and the consequences of those failures (potential injuries). Moreover, many occupational diseases have long latency periods. It is not desirable to wait for harm to occur before judging whether OH&S prevention systems are working or not.[1]

In his book, *The Behavior-based Safety Process*, author Thomas Krause highlights six very important reasons why accident data should not be used as the primary indicator of safety performance:

- The approach is reactive rather than proactive.

- Random variability is misread.

- As a consequence of random variability and its negative effect, management overreacts.

- Safety incentives based on frequency rates amount to false feedback—you may actually be rewarding at-risk behaviors and practices which, through luck, happen to result in low frequency or severity rates.

- The emphasis on frequency rates encourages mere numbers management and lost-time injury record-saving schemes, not improvement in policies, practices, systems, procedures, or risk-taking behavior.

- The net result of the first five factors results in an erosion of the credibility of the safety management system effort.[2]

Performance-Based Measurement

If you want to start changing the existing culture of your organization toward what the authors call an *achievement-based culture®*, the following examples help define what to look for and how to go about implementing a performance-based management system (including behavior-based observations and sampling, perception surveys, strategic planning and action plans, audits, and performance measurement systems).

Performance management measure options can include:

1. objective measures, such as a sound level, dust level, or temperature level reading

2. subjective measures, such as opinions on the quality of housekeeping or maintenance or the adequacy of how "safe" a particular work application may be being carried out in the absence of the no-work method standard

3. quantitative measures, such as an audit score, or an alternative measurement score which uses a standard set of numbers, or scale of numbers. These measures need to be accurate for an assessment of performance over time

4. qualitative measures, such as a description of a condition or situation, such as the effectiveness of management meetings, training course with a rating scale, or the efforts of a joint OH&S committee

Whatever measurement technique employed by your organization, you need to make sure it is meaningful, understandable, accurate, and can be used to help improve specific safety performance areas or general safety culture.

Performance Measurement Examples
- Systematic inspections of the workplace using a standardized checklist approach, then checking the conditions against established standards

- Safety tours and observations of the workplace, work practices, or physical conditions

- Audits or other similar assessments of your safety system

- Observation techniques of conditions or practices (can include various equipment standards or personal practices or compliance to work methods, rules, or standards)

- Degree of risk management improvement

- Safety improvement targets—have they been met/reached/achieved

- Number of safety improvement suggestions made by staff

Defining Your Management System

What's in a name? Plenty, especially when you look at the jargon and language that management system practitioners have been fond of using over the years to demonstrate to others how much we (management system practitioners) know about management systems and how much they (rank and file and management) don't know. All cynicism aside, the language that we use in our day-to-day dealing with others has the potential to speak in a positive way to many of the issues that require special attention. With the world around us becoming more complex and fast-paced everyday, simply keeping up is a major challenge. Keeping up to the point of having some impact on the pace of change is even a greater challenge, in light of all the competing agendas most organizations and management system practitioners have to deal with on a day-to-day basis.

What we say, how it's said, and the content of our spoken and written words can very often mean the difference between various levels of understanding or confusion. While many still refer to their safety system as a "program," the safety programs are actually pieces of the system which, when required, may be changed, added, or deleted as the priorities of their system change. In order to define your OH&S system, it's important to first describe exactly what your system will be comprised of (i.e., what are the health and safety "programs" that you will use in your system). Let's first look again at the definition of a system.

Management Systems Defined (for the Record)
- A system is defined by identifying all interrelated processes and their associated interdependencies.

- A system is managed as a system of interrelated processes.

- A system is improved by continuous measuring and evaluating all related processes.

Depending on the industry you're in, the risks associated with that industry, and the regulatory environment within which your business operates, your system may look drastically different than that of a fellow management system practitioner. Let's consider a typical safety management system as an example. Generally speaking, part of your OH&S system can be defined to come under a number of headings that help in determining which OH&S "programs" fall under the system. For example, one aspect of your OH&S system could be classed under risk management. Another can be accident/incident investigating and reporting. Another may be a safety meeting. You can continue to grow and build upon your respective programs until you have compiled for yourself a rather lengthy array of OH&S programs. Then it's time to break these programs down into their respective system headings. For example, under the corporate heading of the XYZ Company's OH&S management system, you can identify a leadership and administration section, an investigation and analysis section, a compliance section, an emergency response section, and so on. Here's a practical exercise. Underneath these respective sections, you can plot or graph, for visual impact, the various OH&S programs that comprise your entire OH&S management system. This visual depiction of your OH&S system can also be a great tool in explaining to management, or anyone else for that matter, exactly how the pieces of your system fit together or integrate with other management systems in your business.

Performance Measurement and Safety Management Systems

While systems approaches have been used for years in manufacturing processes, only recently has the idea about management systems, or more specifically, safety systems, come into practical use. If we were to apply a typical "closed loop" management system model to occupational health and safety, we could use the typical plan, organize, direct, and control scenario, as depicted in countless management textbooks throughout the years. If you would like to see this model depicted, simply draw a circle and place each of the management functions at each quarter of the outside of the circle.

The piece, which would make this system complete from a safety management perspective, would be a prevention function. Simply add this function in the middle of your circle and draw a broken line from the prevention function to each of the management functions on your model. The logic of adding the prevention function to the management model is to include a preventative, rather than simply a reactive, corrective, or adaptive aspect to your safety management system. The aspect of a prevention function in any management system is to add a stabilizing function to the system. In terms of problem-solving and root cause analysis, the prevention aspect of your management system helps facilitate effective root cause analysis as part of the problem-solving or investigation process. This helps ensure that more than workers' behaviors get addressed as part of the problem-solving model or puzzle.

Measuring Performance

The other benefit that comes from integrating a prevention aspect into your management system model, or by designing a comprehensive safety management system, is that it helps in short- and long-term strategic planning, program delivery, and cost-benefit analysis. Additionally, it provides a sound means of developing your standards for due diligence, if you have concerns that your system may be subject to close examination by regulators. As with any approach to due diligence, you can typically follow two approaches. You can do some "stuff" in safety, run some "safety programs" in the hope that they will address risks and hazards, coin some benign slogans, ask people to be safe, put up some posters, and hope that your efforts are meeting the mark. Or you can strategically plan how your OH&S system is to be structured, how it will roll out, how the pieces will fit together, and how all the pieces, taken together, work synergistically to enhance and heighten your prevention efforts. Why? Because whether you like it or not, if you should be faced with the unfortunate situation of being charged with a serious offense under safety legislation in Canada (see Criminal Code of Canada), you will be forced to demonstrate that you took *all steps reasonable, under the circumstances*, in addressing the potential for the accident or injury not to have happened. By and large, employers are not punished for the errors of their workers or others working on behalf of the employer, but for failing to set up the necessary system(s) intended and designed to prevent such incidents and injuries from happening in the first place.

Audit for Effectiveness

Another benefit of having a clearly defined, graphically represented management system becomes clear during the audit process. The development of your audit methodology can, and should, be patterned after *your* management system. There are too many generic audits available that you can use, but you have to ensure that whichever audit methodology you use, you're auditing the effectiveness of *your* management system, not a system for some auto manufacturing plant in the United States, a pulp and paper mill in New Brunswick, or a fish plant in Newfoundland and Labrador (unless your industry happens to be in one of those sectors). If you're in the petrochemical business, your audit methodology needs to evaluate the effectiveness of your oil and gas business realities, including process safety, as well as other compliance requirements and risk-reducing strategies. Generic audit systems just won't do. They have to be able to be tailored to meet your business and regulatory realities. Anything less will give you less than an accurate picture of your management system, including strengths and weaknesses, and select opportunities for improvement.

The benefit in clearly defining your management system is that you can use the same pattern or "template" to model your management system audit—one should complement, and ideally enhance, the other. Management system development need not be a complicated process. While the size of your system can be complex and comprehensive, depending on the size of your business or the risks associated with its undertaking, it's simply a matter of defining the work to be done, how it's to be done, who's going to do it, and how it's going to be managed. Put it down on paper, graph the important parts, and you've got a visual representation of your management system.

When making presentations to senior management, a picture can be worth a thousand words, so the graphical representation of your management system can go a long way in helping market and promote internal management improvement strategies.

Measurement of Leading Indicators

Many management system practitioners have come to realize that traditional forms of system measurement have serious deficiencies. For example, typical measures of safety performance that have been used to indicate the levels of safe performance—lost-time injuries, frequency and severity, accident costs, and such—on initial examination, would appear to give a good indication of safety performance. The presumption is that if these numbers are low, they indicate a lack of accidents or injuries, therefore, good safety performance.

The weakness of these conventional, after-the-fact accident and injury statistics is that an incident or injury first has to occur in order to have any reliable indicator of performance. This is nothing more than a lesson in bean counting. It tells you nothing about system improvement opportunities or prevention strategies. Accident and injury indicators (including frequency and severity rates) are failure measures. They have their focus on the negative. It's like measuring quality nonconformances or environmental spills. They may be informative and useful, but they are simply a record of your failures. Even sports teams maintain a balance of leading and lagging indicators (wins and losses).

While these result measures are important, they have some severe limitations. They can be used for comparison purposes, but that comparison is still based on failures recorded by your management system as compared with your performance and that of others. And you need to wait until you have a statistically reliable number of these indicators, tracked over a reliable time frame, to give you an accurate picture of your performance. So what should you measure? Or perhaps more accurately, what else can you measure?

A recent trend has been to use management system audits, but these too have limitations. While they are a better form of measurement and have been deemed to be an indication of a higher standard of care from a due-diligence perspective, they have some practical limitations. They are typically performed infrequently, with various schedules for delivery and cycle time, and they very seldom prescribe an ongoing method of measurement to ensure the issues identified for improvement are being managed effectively.

Usually, another management system audit has to be conducted to determine progress or improvement or to determine whether the audit recommendations have been implemented. Indeed, even the behavioral approach to safety (regardless of your personal philosophy on the topic), with its emphasis on at-risk or unsafe behaviors or work actions, can be deemed a more proactive approach to measuring safety, especially if we accept a general definition of safety as being acceptable risk.

The Measurement of Process

One of the key axioms of business is "It is very difficult to manage what you can't measure." Another popular business phrase states, "What gets measured gets done." For these reasons and others, applying the principles of sound performance management is essential for a safety system committed to ongoing improvement.

When we start to critically examine just what it is we should be measuring in our management systems, we quickly come to a central question: if safety, quality, and environmental management is important, and the issues surrounding the minimization of risk or improvement in customer quality have their logic rooted in the actions of people in the organization (people at all levels), what's important to measure? Emphasis needs to be changed from the reactive to the proactive.

It's important that measures for quality, safety, and environmental protection be integrated into the strategic plan of each and every business. If there is a risk to the ability of a business to remain competitive and continue to make a profit, measures from a quality, safety, and environmental perspective need to be used that will not only identify where problems are likely to exist but also will tell how well and effective prevention activities are being managed.

Rather than focus on what has already happened, current and future management system performance measures must focus on improvement of core quality, safety, and environmental prevention strategies. That's easy to say, but how do you start changing your existing measurement culture from one that has depended on failure rates and nonconformances as the key performance indicators to one that actively manages performance improvement efforts on a day-to-day basis and offers achievement-based performance feedback?

Strategic Performance Improvement and Measurement Process

The primary objective of performance measurement is to accurately measure how well the organization is accomplishing its objectives, or some other goal or target. Performance measurement can be used to assist in guiding organizational change and performance improvement. When we look at this concept from a management systems perspective, we get a different take on exactly what must be measured and managed in order for management system performance to improve.

There are a number of important steps that you and your organization should first consider before embarking on a strategic safety performance improvement process.

What's Important, and Why?

Before implementing a performance improvement system, strategic planning should ideally take place to determine what you want to measure, and why. You must seriously ask the question, "What do we want to measure in our health, safety, environmental management, and quality management system, and why?" You also need to ask, "What are we going to do with this information once we are able to capture it?" Ideally, the information you track and measure should be used to allow you to prescribe performance improvement actions, or to reinforce or reward exceptional performance. Once your strategic plan is developed, performance measurements can be the basis for assessing whether this strategy is being achieved.

Performance Measurement Plan

The next step in the process is to determine how the measurement system is to be developed and how the system will track ongoing management system initiatives. What you track and how you will track it will be logical extensions of your strategic plan. A senior-level management team should undertake this step, and the team should consider the needs of the entire organization in the establishment of the system. This team should consider such factors as measures for success, key performance indicators and their relative importance, and how the information is to be used once it becomes available. This group should be responsible, through consultation and performance management objectives, for laying the foundation for the measurement model and eventual recognition opportunities.

Establish Performance Measures, Targets, or Standards

Deciding what you want to measure and why is one of the most important aspects of the measurement process. It is a critical stage of the evaluation process that seeks to answer the questions, "What do we want to measure, why, and how important is it to us?" This stage of the process will be critical to the success of your system. At this point, a family of measures should be identified, with a critical evaluation of how these measures fit your entire management system. Also critical at this stage is the establishment of specific performance indicators. This involves the development of operational definitions that are specific, agreed upon, and capable of being measured. And the measures are assigned a weight, or value of importance, based on your priorities and values.

Example: Measure the Quality of Your Management System   Let's say that one of the key measures identified through your strategic planning is hazard and risk analysis. This element of your management system has been deemed to be important, and you want to establish a system of ongoing measurement to determine whether it's effective. The first step is to define your standards for risk assessment (when and where they are to be done, by whom, and how often), and then determine exactly what is it that you are going to measure to determine whether the system of risk assessments is working or not. This is not an audit in the traditional sense. This is a system of ongoing appraisal of how well you're managing risk assessment activities.

The following are examples of some of the performance indicators you might use for your risk assessment system:[3]

Safety Performance Measurement: Risk and Hazard Analysis System

- Standards are developed for risk or hazard management—50 percent

- Jobs are assessed and evaluated for risks or hazards—20 percent

- Risk or hazard management is used in job training sessions—10 percent

- Risk or hazard management is used in safety meetings—10 percent

- Employees assist in the identification of risks or hazards—10 percent

Once you have determined that these are the measures you will assess, it's then a simple matter of determining what is the best way in which these performance measures are to be tracked and how will they be valued. One of the more common ways is to assign all measures a total score of 100 percent and assign each measure a different percentage (or weight) based on the value of these measures to your organization. This will have been accomplished at steps 2 and 823 by the strategic planning team.

As you can see from the sample, the total of scores for all the measures associated with the family of risk and hazard analysis is 100 percent. This value system for the individual measures is based on what a typical organization may define as important, with "standards developed for risk and hazard analysis" being the most important and weighted at 50 percent to reflect its importance. All other measures in that family are also weighted, based on value or importance.

The key part of the measurement process is tracking on a daily, weekly, monthly, or yearly basis how the organization is performing, compared to its own standards for risk and hazard analysis. These indicators can be tracked simply by modifying existing data entry forms used by the organization to manage these management system elements. Then assign a weight or rating for each of the measures and score them appropriately.[4]

A key part of the performance measurement system is having a reliable information management system or database to manage this information for ease of data entry and accuracy of reporting. The use of a software application is recommended as a necessity to help manage this system.

The number and types of performance measurements can be as many and varied as needed. Use best-practice reports and industry research to design your safety management system to be as wide-ranging or as simple as you wish.

Establish a Performance Baseline

Once performance measures are in place, establish a baseline. This will enable you, through the collection of performance measurement data, to measure how effective the system is in achieving its critical success indicators.

Use the Measurement Information

Now simply use the information you have collected to determine your performance, and see how your management team reacts. As you can see, the measurement of risk and hazard management initiatives is not dependent on having an accident or injury, or any other type of nonconformance. You are measuring the effectiveness of the *process* you have defined for effective risk management, not how many or how few injuries or nonconformances you have.

If you are doing a good job in managing risk and customer expectations, you will have a better indicator of your management system performance. The potential for these accidents and injury statistics to increase or decrease is being managed, and this is what performance management and measurement are all about. If you want to offer a performance recognition option, you now have that opportunity based on prevention activities, not mere injury statistics.

Safety Performance Measurement Options

If you really want to turn your safety performance measurement and recognition system into an *achievement-based system*®, rather than a failure-based system, consider some practical measurement and reward alternatives. They take the emphasis off accidents and injuries and raise the bar on behavior-based safety due to the fact that they assess not only the behaviors of many people in the business (not simply workers) but also the goals, performance targets, standards, and achievements of management as well. Additionally, variations on these performance and achievement themes can be part of any systems audit that you decide may be necessary to complement an achievement-based safety model.[5]

From Theory to Reality

What you determine to be important to track and measure should be a direct consequence of the priorities, values, practices, and activities that your management team feels will add the most value to the management system improvement effort. They lend a whole new dimension to the phrase, "what gets measured gets done." Or preferably, "what gets measured gets managed," because what gets managed stands a better chance of getting recognized, reinforced, and repeated.

1. HSEQ (Health, Safety, Environment, and Quality) Objective Setting
   - HSEQ objectives in place.
   - HSEQ objectives reviewed periodically.
   - HSEQ objectives are being met.
   - HSEQ objectives shared with employees.
   - HSEQ objectives are both statistical- (target) and performance- (activity) based.

2. Root Cause Analysis for Nonconformances/Accidents/Incidents, etc.
   - Root cause analysis completed as required.
   - Root cause analysis identified the cause(s) of the accident.
   - Corrective action strategies to prevent recurrence identified.
   - Corrective action strategies implemented or are in the process of being implemented.

3. HSEQ Committes
   - Committee(s) meet as required.
   - Minutes are posted in the workplace as required.
   - Equal representation of worker and management representatives.
   - Action arising from the meeting documented.
   - Action arising from meeting completed or are in the process of being completed.

4. Management Training and Development
   - Training needs for management identified.
   - Training courses for management delivered.
   - Senior and middle management have received instruction in legislative compliance, due diligence, and quality management system issues.

5. Inspection and Maintenance
   - Inspection/maintenance schedule in place.
   - Schedule being followed.
   - Inspection/maintenance procedures identify deficiencies or compliance.
   - Inspection/maintenance deficiencies being followed up, or compliance recognized.
   - Follow-up completed or is in the process of being completed.

6. HSEQ Meetings
   - Schedule developed for HSEQ meetings.
   - Agenda posted prior to HSEQ meetings.
   - Adequate topics prepared/available for HSEQ meeting.
   - Current HSEQ performance communicated/updated to staff at meeting.
   - Corrective action from HSEQ meeting completed or is in the process of being completed.

7. HSEQ Audits
   - HSEQ audits conducted as per audit schedule.
   - Nonconformances identified, or compliance recognized.
   - Corrective action initiated on audit deficiencies.
   - Corrective action completed on audit deficiencies.
   - Compliance recognized.

8. Personal Protective Equipment
   - Personal protective equipment needs identified.

- Appropriate personal protective equipment available for job task.
- Appropriate personal protective equipment used as required for job tasks.
- Personal protective equipment maintained appropriately.
- Personal protective equipment stored properly when not in use.

9. Hazard and Risk Analysis
   - Jobs assessed and evaluated for risks and hazards.
   - Standards developed for risk management.
   - Risk management used in job training.
   - Risk management used in job planning.
   - Employees assist in identification of job risks.

10. Fall Protection
    - Falling risks evaluated, using hazard and risk analysis.
    - Fall protection standards in place.
    - Fall protection equipment available.
    - Fall protection equipment being used as required.
    - Fall protection equipment properly stored and maintained.

11. HSEQ Performance Standards—Managerial
    - Standards for managerial HSEQ activities defined.
    - Standards define frequency of HSEQ activities.
    - Standards define responsibilities and accountability.
    - Standards define how managerial HSEQ performance is to be measured.
    - Performance standards evaluated with each managerial employee.

12. Emergency Response
    - Emergency response plans in place.
    - Emergency response plans address risks identified in hazard and risk analysis.
    - First aid and CPR training needs identified.
    - First aid and CPR training conducted as required.

13. HSEQ Promotion
    - Promotional campaigns target specific risk, environmental, or quality factors.
    - Promotional campaigns developed with employee input.

14. Regulatory Compliance System
    - Regular assessment of regulatory compliance conducted.

- Regulatory compliance issues discussed at all management meetings.
- Managerial staff receives regular updates on regulatory compliance.
- Managerial staff receives instruction on due-diligence issues.

15. Prework Planning ("Tool Box" Talks)
    - Prework plans completed as required.
    - Key risk factors identified and minimized through prework plan.
    - Job completed as per prework plan.
    - Prework plan approved by supervisor on-site.

16. Safe Behavior Observation System
    - Safe (at-risk) behavior performance standards developed.
    - Safe behavior observation conducted as required.
    - Safe behaviors noted and recognized for positive reinforcement.
    - At-risk behaviors noted and corrected.
    - Acceptable behaviors documented and reinforced.

17. Contractor HSEQ Compliance
    - Contractor HSEQ policy in place.
    - Contractor HSEQ plan defined for project.
    - HSEQ expectations of contractors defined and shared with contractor.
    - Contractor HSEQ performance evaluated.
    - Contractor performing project in compliance with contractor HSEQ plan.

18. Housekeeping
    - Housekeeping assessment conducted as required.
    - Exemplary housekeeping noted and recognized.
    - Housekeeping deficiencies identified.
    - Corrective action initiated or implemented.

19. Workers' Compensation
    - Claims initiated as required.
    - Workers' compensation paperwork completed as required.
    - Claim managed as per company policies and/or regulatory requirements.[6]

The primary focus here is to develop and implement a strategic safety performance measurement system that will facilitate any type of performance recognition option you deem desirable. The actual type of award may not be as important, in the practical sense, compared to what you actually decide needs to be measured. There is a difference between making performance improvement measurements in order to determine how effective your business is operating and measuring for reward or recognition purposes. The phenomena known as contest contamination needs to be avoided.

Additionally, if you want to move your safety management system from a failure- or statistic-based system to an achievement-based model or a performance-based system, the following one hundred performance measures, profiled in the September 1995 *Industrial Safety and Hygiene* news, offer many opportunities for creativity:

1. Total workers' compensation costs

2. Average cost per claim

3. Costs per human-hour

4. OSHA 200 logs

5. Industry ranking

6. Behavior observation data

7. Benchmarking other companies

8. Employee perception surveys

9. Frequency of all injuries/illnesses

10. Severity of all injuries/illnesses

11. Lost-time accidents

12. Investigations completed on time

13. Investigation identifies causes

14. Investigation identifies action plan

15. Action plans implemented

16. Safety meetings held as scheduled

17. Agenda promoted in advance

18. Safety records updated and posted

19. Inspections conducted as scheduled

20. Inspection findings brought to closure

21. Management safety communications

22. Management safety participation

23. Near-miss/near-hit reports

24. Discipline/violation reports

25. Self-audits for regulatory compliance

26. Contractor injury/illness statistics

27. Total manufacturing process incidents

28. Total transportation incidents

29. Rate of employee suggestions/complaints

30. Resolution of suggestions/complaints

31. Vehicle accidents per mile driven

32. Safety committee activities

33. Management initiatives

34. Respiratory protection audit

35. Hearing conservation audit

36. Spill control audit

37. Emergency response audit

38. Toxic exposure monitoring audit

39. Ventilation audit

40. Lab safety audit

41. Health/medical services audit

42. Hazard communication audit

43. Ergonomics audit

44. Blood-borne pathogens audit

45. Housekeeping audit

46. Job safety analyses

47. Lock-out/tag-out audit

48. Confined spaces audit

49. Machine guarding audit

50. Electrical safety audit

51. Vehicle safety audit

52. Fire protection audit

53. Employee participation rates

54. Employee housekeeping

55. Employee safety awareness

56. Employee at-risk behavior

57. Supervisor/manager participation

58. Supervisor/manager communication

59. Supervisor/manager enforcement

60. Supervisor/manager safety emphasis

61. Supervisor/manager safety awareness

62. Injury/illness cases reported on time

63. Statistical reports issued on time

64. Ratio of safety and health staff to workforce

65. Safety and health spending per employee

66. Titles in safety and health library

67. Technical assistance bulletins issued

68. Policies and procedures updated on time

69. Wellness program participation rates

70. Security audits

71. Emergency drills conducted as planned

72. Percent employees trained in CPR/first aid

73. Absenteeism rates

74. Productivity per employee rates

75. Production error rates

76. Incidence of workplace violence

77. Incidence of accidental releases

78. Employee exit interviews

79. Employee focus groups

80. Community outreach/public safety initiatives

81. Off-the-job safety initiatives

82. Insurance/consultant reports

83. Reports of peer support for safety

84. Certifications of health and safety personnel

85. Percent safety goals achieved

86. Training conducted as scheduled

87. Safety training test scores

88. Statistical tracking of programs

89. Statistical process control

90. System safety analysis

91. Contractor safety activities

92. Positive reinforcement activities

93. OSHA audit—no citations

94. OSHA audit—citations, no fines

95. Willful violations

96. Serious or repeat violations

97. Other-than-serious violations

98. Total dollar amount of penalties

99. Average time to abate reported hazard

100. Average time to respond to complaint

The value of these achievement-based safety criteria is that they can be used to help set performance objectives for everyone in your company, from the most senior executives to each and every hourly worker. They can help structure your own achievement-based performance model to suit your unique corporate culture, safety goals, and objectives.

These measures can be used to complement one another, so that senior and middle management have to support the line in order to achieve their objectives and workers can see a very definite relationship between their efforts and the corporate direction and philosophy of the business. An achievement-based performance model does not thrive on the exclusion of one group over any other, but it is the basis for a high-performance system that can energize and strengthen your entire prevention system.[7]

CHAPTER FIVE

THE INTERNAL RESPONSIBILITY SYSTEM FOR MANAGEMENT SYSTEM ACCOUNTABILITY

There is one management system concept from Canada that the authors are both pleased and proud to be able to profile in greater detail. While many may have difficulty identifying a uniquely Canadian concept for integrated management systems (including the authors!), with a cursory nod to the Europeans, Canada is able to point to the internal responsibility system for workplace safety as a model for all management system advocates to learn and study in greater detail. And while it's been said in some circles that the safety-quality relationship are sometimes the opposite side of the same coin, the internal responsibility system, in the opinion of the authors, holds great potential for integrated management system performance, especially in consideration of an integrated management system accountability scheme.

It's been said that as a profession, safety and quality practitioners have some of the best clichés around. When the cliché "safety and quality is everybody's responsibility" is examined with any reasonable degree of critical logic, it becomes very clear that if all we continue to say is that safety is everybody's responsibility in general, then it is highly likely that the potential for it to become nobody's responsibility in particular is a strong probability. And just what does "work smarter, not harder" really mean? And if quality is job #1, what is job #2, or #3? You get the point. Sometimes these slogans and clichés become so banal as to mean absolutely nothing.

Just as in any reasoned approach to a team-based focus for business management, unless and until specific responsibilities are defined and assigned, it will be difficult for the respective members of the "team" to know exactly what is expected of them, when, and why, or whether they've performed to expectations. This is why the Canadian version of the internal responsibility system appeals to the authors, and we trust the following rationale will make sense for your integrated management system.

Under the Canadian concept of the IRS (Internal Responsibility System—not Internal Revenue Service) the emphasis on the means for safe production recognizes that all workers, be they management or hourly worker, need to have a crystal-clear understanding of their role in the management system. Typically, many in senior management are quite good at espousing the motherhood rhetoric of safety and quality, but if you were to conduct an audit or interview of these senior management staff and ask them, "What do you do on a day-to-day basis to demonstrate your commitment to safety, quality, and environmental management, or to help promote and integrate a positive management system culture?," what do you think the typical answers might be?

If your organization has taken the time to rationalize and define clear expectations, responsibilities, and accountabilities, you will start to get a good idea on how to go about setting up a meaningful system of responsibilities for your management system. Here's a small (or large) test. Take each and every job position and description in your existing business and see if you can define clear responsibilities for safety, quality, and environmental management that not only you but others in the organization will agree with and understand. Take this one step further. Take the following job titles and ask yourself, "Have we defined all the appropriate safety, quality, and environmental management system responsibilities for these jobs?"

- president

- vice presidents

- managers and directors

- supervisors

- workers

Unless and until you conduct this exercise and are able to sell the outcome to key decision makers in your organization, many people in your organization will still feel that safety, quality, and environmental management is the job of the staff management system professional or practitioner in question.

And don't forget to define the responsibilities for the QHSE (quality, health, safety, and environment) manager and staff as well. Staff QHSE practitioners play a "contributive role" in the internal responsibility system. Management and workers play a "direct role." There's a big difference between the two. But unless and until you define clear and easily understood QHSE responsibilities, confusion in your QHSE management system can become a daily reality. This is not to say that the QHSE practitioner does not play a very strong

Table 5.1. **Integrated Management System Accountability Framework**

Responsibilities	Worker	First-Line Supervisor	Superintendent	Manager	Vice President	President and CEO
Nature of work	Process material	Assign tasks	Schedule work	Interpret objectives and plan operations	Determine objectives	Establish purpose
Responsibility of people	Direct helpers	Instruct and develop workers	Develop supervisors	Select and develop supervisors	Select and develop staff	Select VP
Responsibility of work performance	Use knowledge and skill and exercise initiative	Direct work performance within clearly defined job specifications	Specify duties and responsibilities and define authority	Assign duties and responsibilities and delegate authority	Determine functions	Delegate operating authority
Responsibility for direction of work	Carry out work in a manner consistent with approved practices and procedures	Carry out duties in a manner consistent with policies and procedures and philosophy of enterprise	Carry out duties in a manner consistent with policies and procedures and philosophy of enterprise	Interpret policies and procedures in light of business philosophy in administration of business activities	Establish business philosophy, develop operating policies, and standardize administrative procedures	Determine business philosophy and procedures

(continued)

Table 5.1. (continued)

Responsibilities	Worker	First-Line Supervisor	Superintendent	Manager	Vice President	President and CEO
Responsibility for relations with people	Work cooperatively with others	Coordinate performance of tasks	Coordinate work program(s)	Coordinate supporting services	Conduct the operation of the enterprise in a manner compatible with legislated requirement and social trends	Determine policies to make the purpose of the enterprise compatible with legislative requirement and social trends
Responsibilities for facilities and equipment	Use facilities, machines, and tools	Provide adequate tools and equipment	Provide adequate services and machines	Make provision for necessary facilities, machines, and equipment	Obtain capital goods	Authorize capital expenditures
Responsibilities for conditions of work	Maintain standard conditions	Implement standard conditions	Provide facilities for standardized conditions	Set standards of work performance and working conditions	Determine standards of work performance and working conditions	Determine policies for the operation of the enterprise

NOTE: This is a *sample* of the internal responsibility system structure for the performance of work, based on the model profiled by the Ham Commission.

leadership role. He or she does indeed have that role, but we will deal with the issue of leadership in the integrated management system in more detail in the section on leadership.

According to Justice Ham, in the Ham Commission report of 1976, "It is critically important that the managerial system for the performance of work be effective. Table 5.1 was prepared as a model to demonstrate how the duties of all persons in the organization can be interrelated to achieve integration of the responsibilities essential to the effective performance of work."[1] This table will be referred to as the internal responsibility system for the performance of work. The responsibilities associated with the performance of the duties as defined in the columns of table 5.1 must be adequately understood and prepared for if the person is to be able to perform the role effectively and to be held accountable for the identification and correction of the departure from standard conditions. It is management's underlying responsibility to see that this internal responsibility system is effectively in place and in particular that there is open understanding among parties of their duties and responsibilities in the performance of work.[2]

The Canadian system of internal responsibility for occupational health and safety has been patterned, to a degree, on similar systems used in the United Kingdom and various Scandinavian countries. In most developed countries, government regulators have carved out a role as advocates of workers and hold themselves up as being the protectors and benevolent benefactors of workers from a health and safety perspective. However, it's interesting to note that while many in government are sometimes very quick to take the credit when industrial safety performance improves, they are not quite as anxious to step forward and take responsibility for industrial safety performance when it is poor or things are not as positive as they would wish.

The United States may be able to take some lessons from European and Canadian counterparts in terms of safety management strictly from a regulatory responsibility perspective. In Scandinavian countries, the term *self-regulation* (seen by some as an oxymoron) has been guiding the development and implementation of workplace health and safety strategies for years, especially in the offshore oil and gas industry in the harsh and unforgiving offshore environment of the North Sea. While many businesses and government agencies struggle to come up with new and wonderful incentive approaches to get workers to perform some activity to which they may be naturally averse, the system of internal responsibility holds much promise for worker motivation, empowerment, and recognition from a health and safety perspective. Indeed, the authors suggest behavior-based safety advocates can enhance the value of behavioral approaches to workplace safety through a variation of the IRS concept.

In the internal control system, the name of the game is ongoing system documentation, reviews, and regular input from management and workers. The whole thrust behind the idea is that workers and management participate in the development of the system that serves their own best interests. The core of the internal responsibility system is that you have to continuously work at creating a safer environment. This responsibility concept, in the opinion of the authors, holds significant potential for opportunities for improvement for quality and environmental management system performance as well. At the core of the responsibility system is ownership. If I have a vested interest or stake in something, chances are I will be more inclined to take more personal responsibility for management system initiatives.

With a heavy emphasis on the principle of employee involvement and ownership as part of the internal control system, Norwegian companies implementing this approach have noted increased safety and health awareness, in addition to improved risk assessment in their offshore oil and gas industry.

One of the potential benefits of the Canadian approach to the internal responsibility system is that in some jurisdictions, it spells out actual responsibilities for occupational health and safety, from the CEO and other management and supervisory personnel to workers. The value of this clear definition of safety responsibilities is that it can accommodate both high-level and lower-level performance improvement approaches. While many approaches to safety management have the worker as the only focus, the utilization of an effective internal responsibility system can ensure that, strategically speaking, all human resources within the organization play a part and make a contribution to improved safety performance. In addition to safety management, the more clear the responsibilities for managing quality and environmental management system initiatives, the more definitive the measurement of the effectiveness, or conversely, the failure of the management systems.

What some believe to be the definitive study of the value of the internal responsibility system in Canada resulted from the *Report of the Royal Commission of the Health and Safety of Workers in Mines*, commonly known in Canadian circles as the Ham Commission report. The June 1976 report was a landmark piece of work for the future of workplace health and safety in Canada. To investigate the criticism organized labor levied toward government and industry, the Ham Commission found it beneficial to use the concept of the internal responsibility system, which encompassed, in the opinion of the commission, the roles of all parties involved.[3]

The opportunity for the management system community to learn from this seminal report can be summarized in the following analysis of the Ham Commission: "Whether in the home or the factory, on the highway, or in a mine, there is no attainable state of absolute health and safety. There are levels of risk accepted or tolerated to a degree by the parties concerned. Mines can only exist where economically viable operations can be conducted. Within operating mines, the acceptable levels of risk are determined by:

- the quality and kind of industrial management and supervision

- the degree of participation and commitment of employees, individually and collectively, in labor unions and otherwise

- the state of social expectation and concern in mining communities and the public at large

- the measure of political attention as expressed in legislation, in the related governmental administrative practices for monitoring compliance, and in the provision for compensation

- the combined effectiveness of the above parties in operating as a system."[4]

While Ham was perhaps not contemplating any quality or environmental management issues beyond the scope of his defined study, his work and that of his commission holds significant potential for those involved in the day-to-day management of integrated management systems. And while most of us in the management system field usually reference our own personal guru for the sound bite or cliché that will neatly sum up how we view our approach to management systems, I can think of no greater summary than that of Justice Ham, who quite succinctly noted:

> The apparently common view that the great majority of accidents are the direct result of nothing more than unsafe acts or unsafe conditions is, in the Commission's opinion, too restricted a view of the human problem of accidental injuries (or quality problems or environmental concerns). Workmen and their supervisors at every level may act unwisely, but they do so within a system for the performance of work whose responsibility it is to set clear and supervised standards of what is expected. Within such a system workers have a clear obligation to perform work by standard procedures, and supervision has the responsibility to see that standard conditions of work, tools and equipment are maintained. . . . Any internal system of direct responsibility will be imperfect and requires audit, not because of any inherent defect in form but because it is a human organization in which conditions of work and concern for the well being of persons create grounds for tension.[5]

The bottom line . . . accountability.

No matter what the technical makeup of your internal management system, its ability to thrive and perform without dysfunction will be dependent to some degree of the ability of all the internal parties being able to work together, both individually and collectively, to achieve the desired management system objectives. As we know, organizations are comprised of people, and not all the people in your organization may share your passion or vision of an integrated management system. And they may have different agendas that, intentional or unintentional, may work in opposition to the management system objectives.

Workplace 2000: The Quality/Safety Relationship

There have been many articles written over the years that examined the relationship between the safety and quality management disciplines. As noted, it has often been said that safety and quality are sometimes the opposite sides of the same coin and often complement one another. While many of these articles were theoretical or speculative in nature, some have clearly hit the mark. With his kind permission, Tom Smith of Mocal, Inc., has provided the authors with an opportunity to provide the readers of this book with one of those "on the mark" articles.

According to Smith, the safety profession seems to be fading from the prominence it once held in the 1980s to a lesser role in management. Safety is still handled more as an afterthought as demonstrated by the events of the *Challenger* and subsequent *Columbia* disasters. There is now an emphasis on understanding culture and its important impact on safety, but progress there has been very slow.

Lean manufacturing and reengineering has certainly taken its toll on how many people are employed as safety professionals as management cuts people to satisfy the numbers. Unfortunately, the reduction of safety managers and staff was not in response to a change of philosophy of empowering workers to improve safety but merely to reduce overhead.

There has been a huge loss of manufacturing jobs in the United States. Consider just a few of the facts and figures. An article in *Managing Automation* in May 2004, stated:

> An estimated 2.8 million U.S. manufacturing jobs have been lost over the last 42 months. Manufacturing employment in the U.S. is now at its lowest level in 45 years. Manufacturing production and new hiring remain stagnant, even as the economic recovery gains momentum. None of the 308,000 jobs that were created in March were in manufacturing, according to the Labor Department. And there has been a seemingly unstoppable decline in manufacturing's overall economic contribution. Since 1999, the percentage of U.S. gross domestic product attrib-

uted to manufacturing has slid from 16% to 14%. Manufacturing's share of the national income—29% in 1950—declined to 15% in 2000.

It doesn't take a rocket scientist to figure out that traditional middle management jobs such as safety manager or director are no longer high priorities in the boardroom. Sadly, I don't see enough of a transformation in safety management I advocated back in 1996. Deep down inside, American managers believe they can delegate their responsibility for safety directly to the workers. These managers honestly believe that is the best way to manage safety. The primary focus of safety management for these people is still on the behavior of the individual employee rather than improving the system.

Imagine taking this approach for quality. Stating the main reason for defects or poor customer satisfaction is the fault of the workers. Many managers have not been able to make the connection or see the relationship between safety and quality I was trying to explain in this article. Safety, like quality, is an outcome of the system of management. How a company hires, trains, treats, and respects employees determines its safety performance to a much greater degree than meeting OSHA regulations or internal company safety audits.

I'm truly perplexed by the lack of adoption of quality theory by many safety managers. Although, I have to say, it's not their fault. Pick up any safety journal and you will still find that the majority of articles focus on traditional safety methods and techniques couched in the theory of quality. I do believe safety managers are still the key people to add value to any organization by leading the transformation of management from a command-and-control model to continual improvement.

Modern safety managers I work with keep learning about managing in a flat world where bottom-up control is the rule rather then the exception. The transformation of safety in this context focuses on building teams to study and improve the safety system using the same theory, methods, tools, and technology applied in quality efforts such as Six Sigma, Total Quality, Lean Manufacturing, etc.

Manufacturing in the United States is still in a state of crisis and worse, as Dr. Deming said in the early 1990s; we don't know it or won't admit it. The challenge I see in safety management is to advance its ability to serve the customers it is really meant to serve—the people who do the work.

The stories of "Joe" and "Kim" follow; I still meet "Joe" or a variation of him at many companies. I also continue to work and develop more managers who are striving to understand and approach their careers to be like "Kim," which is a much more satisfying and effective way of improving safety. Many safety professionals talk about using the principles of quality methods or continual improvement to manage safety. However, close examination of what they are actually doing reveals that safety management is missing the point. The second wave of the Industrial Revolution is here and has changed safety management methods and personnel.

In early 1993, for the first time since records have been kept, more white-collar employees were unemployed than blue-collar workers. Quality methods have allowed companies to increase quality and productivity with less supervision. Companies have learned how to make products and provide services without multiple layers of middle managers. In fact, many middle management jobs are disappearing forever.

The bureaucracy and hierarchy of centralized management is being attacked and dismantled. The new management system exists not to ensure that managements' orders are executed but to help employees and remove barriers that prevent them from doing their jobs.

Some organizations have learned that bigger is not always better with respect to management. Extra layers often create an organization that is slow to act and change. One can think of many large companies that have lost market share to smaller competitors who were better prepared to satisfy customers. Companies are learning how to be lean and still produce higher quality and quantity. How will safety fit into these organizations?

Management's Job Has Changed

Employees' jobs used to be broken down into the smallest task—no thinking necessary. Instead, management did all of the thinking. This is not a "quality method" approach. Production problems are so vast and complex that everyone within the organization is needed to study and improve the system. What is true for production management is also true for safety management.

Companies are flattening their organizational structure, often by eliminating middle management. Technology is playing a key role in this evolution. Upper managers no longer need staff to gather, tabulate, analyze, and summarize information about operations—they use computers instead. The endangered species list now includes middle managers that advise workers. Safety managers are on this list, as many companies are reducing safety staff along with other middle management departments.

Traditional Safety Management

Consider how one company's safety program is run by Joe, a safety manager trained in the traditional safety management methods taught in colleges and used in most organizations today. His goal is to run an efficient, effective department. To do this, Joe sets up activities to monitor and control employees and supervisors and ensure compliance with company safety rules and regulations.

Much of his time is spent providing government-mandated safety training and conducting safety inspections and audits. He negotiates next year's safety goals with top management. He sets safety standards for employees and tracks their performance, conducts accident investigations, and recommends corrective action to prevent future incidents.

As demands on his time increase, Joe adds staff to help complete training, safety inspections, accident investigations, and data collection. He recruits other managers for the safety committee, which establishes goals via management by objectives. He teaches this process to supervisors, and a mutually agreed-upon goal for accident reduction is set (typically between 5 and 10 percent.)

Joe implements a sophisticated program to collect accident data. Each department is monitored and compared, and changes in monthly rates must be explained. Managers are held accountable for accidents; they in turn hold their employees accountable.

Joe's idea of working upstream is changing employee behavior. To ensure that he is motivating employees to work safely, Joe establishes safety incentive programs, which reward employees or departments that achieve preset safety goals. Typically, the goals are zero accidents for a certain length of time. If goals are reached, gifts or monetary awards are presented at a banquet. If goals are not met, no awards are given, and the program is restarted or replaced.

In short, Joe's idea of a good safety manager is one who establishes an efficient, effective safety management system. His main responsibilities are:

- monitoring managers and employees to ensure they follow his directives correctly

- setting goals for employees

- rating managers for the ability to follow safety instructions

- evaluating employees to see whether they demonstrate safe behaviors

- reeducating workers after an accident and returning them to work; if an employee frequently has accidents, Joe informs management, and that employee is reassigned or replaced if necessary

- providing numbers to show improvement; he explains poor results by identifying those who are ruining the program—this ferrets out the truly poor performers

Quality Safety Management

Contrast Joe's approach with that of Kim, a safety manager who uses quality methods for safety. She feels her job is to facilitate a constant effort—safety does not start and stop depending on the most recent performance. Kim knows that as a manager, she works on the system and the employees work in it. To improve the system's safety performance, Kim knows she needs their knowledge and input.

Kim provides leadership; helping everyone—top management and employees—understand why the company must improve its safety performance. To manage safety using quality methods, she abandons the traditional approach of ensuring compliance with safety specifications, knowing that meeting safety specifications merely guarantees the goal will not be reached.

Kim focuses on underlying causal factors that create the interdependent activities, which allow accidents to occur. She works on critical behaviors of management, realizing that managers control the processes that lead to employee injuries. Rather than replace employees, she strives to change the management-controlled safety system so employees can perform their jobs without fear of injury.

To do this, Kim takes a customer view of safety—employees are her most important customers. She constantly tries to get their voice into the process, which improves safety and productivity. Employees know best where safety improvements should be made.

To Kim, accidents are worse than producing scrap. When an accident occurs, not only do quality and productivity decline but also employee respect for management. She sees safety as an outcome of the system. She understands that events that cause accidents occur randomly, that variation exists in everything—including safety. Each job is different; each employee is unique, making it impossible to design a job for the "average" employee.

To enable management and employees to work together, Kim helps them take a systems view of safety, which uses the common language of statistics. Instead of a mechanistic view of accident causation, they look at accidents as a system outcome. Statistical process control charts provide a new way of looking at accident rates. All employees learn the philosophy of statistical process control and chart their safety performance. These charts show whether accidents are out of control due to special causes or are affected only by random variation. These charts also help supervisors stop blaming employees for accidents and focus efforts on system problems.

Kim establishes teams to identify, rank, and solve production safety problems. These teams do not merely make suggestions about safety improvements, they also use the Plan-Do-Check-Act cycle for safety:

- They use problem-solving tools such as process flowcharts and cause-and-effect diagrams to develop and implement system changes.

- They study these changes and evaluate their effectiveness.

- If ineffective, the team sticks with the problem and makes improvements until its causes are eliminated.

Kim's most important activity is to remove barriers that prevent employees from doing their jobs safely. She does not change their behavior through extrinsic motivators but relies on intrinsic motivators such as pride in their work and self-preservation to keep safety foremost in their minds.

She knows that extrinsic motivators destroy intrinsic motivators, so she does not use safety incentive programs. Her time is better spent making certain real accident causes (poor management) are eliminated. Employees view a safety goal of 5 to 10 percent reduction as "dumb" because it prevents them from improving the system. As customers, they want 100 percent reduction.

Kim does not think of employees as faceless numbers. She knows they are thinkers and creative human beings. She needs and respects their opinions and ideas. Therefore, she does not name a "safe employee of the month" or display "motivational" safety posters. Employees already do that—and more—by themselves. They measure their safety performance and use safety teams to make continual improvements on their own suggestions.

She convinces supervisors that time spent on safety adds value to the company—it not only improves safety, it also increases productivity and quality. Management responds to safety problems in the same way it does to production problems. Employees are trained on problem-solving techniques and given time to apply the PDCA cycle to fix the system. Safety is serious business and is always a win-win situation.

Conclusion

Traditional safety managers accept the system as it is and try to get the most out of it. In contrast, safety managers who use quality methods know that blaming employees for not complying with the rules provides no solution. As a result, they create trust between management and employees. Employees learn that their jobs involve more than just showing up and collecting a paycheck. In addition to normal production responsibilities, they study the safety system and help management solve problems within that system.

Safety professionals must chose between managing safety to "meet specifications" or using quality methods and continual improvement to satisfy safety customers.

These approaches have nothing in common. You can't reconcile them. You must chose one or the other for either one to be effective. Managing to meet safety specifications does not result in continual improvement. At best it maintains the status quo.

Managing safety using quality methods requires a new level of thinking in which employees are viewed as safety problem-solvers, not the reason accidents occur. Management must continue evolving to meet customer demands. Layers of middle management, created to monitor and control employees, are not needed in new management models and will probably never return.

However, someone must manage the safety system. The new safety management model gives this responsibility to those who do the work. These people help gather and analyze data and make decisions that directly impact safety performance.

Using the new approach will help companies achieve a level of safety performance once thought impossible. The question for today's safety professional: Which approach will you chose?[6]

CHAPTER SIX
BEHAVIOR-BASED APPROACHES TO INTEGRATED MANAGEMENT SYSTEMS

In looking at opportunities for maximizing your investment in an integrated management system, the opportunity to integrate practical applications of behavioral approaches to management system practices is a very practical reality for today's management system practitioner.

In the quest for practical behavioral approaches to deal with opportunities for people management in your integrated management system, there are some practical considerations before embarking on that journey. And it may or may not be without controversy. Behavioral safety has both its fair share of advocates and detractors. And while we could spend untold pages going over the pros and cons of the behavioral approach to safety, the authors felt that rather than make behavioral safety just another point of ongoing debate, we would help profile some of the issues surrounding behavioral safety. For those feeling there is a practical application to their existing management system, we offer some opportunities exploring and rationalizing where this synergy can be realized in your integrated management system.

Just as with the topic of whether there is any strategic or business advantage of an integrated management system, you will find as many different opinions and approaches to behavioral safety as there are management system practitioners. Most people who have been exposed to behavioral management usually come down very strongly and articulately on one side of the other in the behavioral debate. We'll leave the selling or rejection of behavior-based safety and behavioral approaches to quality management to those who have a vested interest in its survival or demise; however, we think it is only fair that due to the nature and scope of the many and varied ways in which the people factor is deemed to be an integral part of most safety management systems, at least a cursory profile is warranted.

What Is Behavior-Based Safety?

According to Wikipedia, behavior-based safety (BBS) is the "application of science of behavior change to real-world problems."

The person who advocates a behavioral approach to management systems "focuses on what people do, analyzes why they do it, and then applies a research-supported intervention strategy to improve what people do."[1]

Behavior-based safety systems are not designed to be based on assumptions, personal feeling, and/or common knowledge. To be successful, the behavioral system used must be based on scientific knowledge. A good BBS program will typically consist of:

- common goals—both employee and managerial involvement in the process

- a definition of what is expected—in other words, there are specifically defined and acceptable target behaviors derived from safety assessments or baseline behavioral assessments

- observational data collection—a cornerstone of the behavioral process is the data collected stemming from observations of specific, observable behaviors of workers conducting a specific task

- decisions about how best to proceed based on those data

- feedback to associates being observed

- review[2]

A typical characteristic of the behavioral approach is a review of the performance of the system using the input of many individuals and multilevel teams. Just as the identification and segregation of risk-based behaviors is critical to the success of BBS, so too must the system be able to demonstrate appropriate "safe" attitude adjustment in order to be sustaining. Much of the research referenced by behavioral advocates highlights that it has been proven that "behavior influences attitude and attitude influences behavior." The goal should be small gains over and over again, with the objective being continuous growth and improvement. It is cautioned, however, that behavioral safety is not a magic solution or quick fix. It is a commitment. In other words, don't expect overnight success by putting in another "program" and expecting the program, in and of itself, to be the ultimate solution.[3]

The overall success of any behavioral approach is contingent upon how well it is able to integrate with other management system policies, procedures, and practices, such that it becomes part and parcel of the way a business manages its affairs and is not seen as simply an "add on" of the program of the week. There are numerous commercially available programs on how to implement behavior-based safety programs. They all vary in price, detail, and delivery (and sometimes rhetoric). But the advocated goal is always the same: eliminate injury. A review of much of the scientific publications on behavior-based safety since the mid-1970s to date shows that different approaches exert different effects. Focusing on work groups, in static settings it was demonstrated to be the most efficient at behavior change and injury reduction.[4]

Behavior-based safety is a topic that has been around for a considerably long time, although not without its controversy. Behavioral approaches to safety originated with the work of Herbert William Heinrich.[5]

In the 1930s, Heinrich, an employee of Traveler's Insurance Company, reviewed literally thousands of accident reports completed by investigating supervisors, and from these (some would suggest subjective reports) he came to the conclusion that most accidents, illnesses, and injuries in the workplace are directly attributable to "man-failures," or the unsafe actions of workers. Of the reports Heinrich reviewed, 73 percent classified the accidents as "man-failures"; Heinrich himself reclassified another 15 percent into that category, arriving at the still-cited finding that 88 percent of all accidents, injuries, and illnesses are caused by worker errors. Heinrich's data does not tell why the person did what they did to cause the accident, just that the accident occurred. And the bias upon which some people believe his research was based is further proof of the inaccuracy of this 88 percent assertion. Be that as it may, behavioral approaches to workplace safety explore and examine the actions of people (i.e., the individual involved in the accident) that supposedly caused the accident. It also considers the workplace; the environment, equipment, and procedures; and attitudes.[6]

Heinrich and the Basis for Modern Safety Management

A major study by the Australian government explores Heinrich's research in some detail. The exploration, in a review of the literature on health and safety management systems, notes, "Heinrich's major research study concerned the causes of accidents and comprised a subjective assessment of the accident cause in 75,000 accident insurance cases. He concluded that 88 per cent of accidents resulted from 'unsafe acts' and 10 per cent from 'unsafe conditions,' making a total of 98 per cent judged to be preventable, with the remaining 2 per cent judged as unpreventable. Heinrich advocated a multi-disciplinary approach to safety, focused upon engineering, psychology, management and 'salesmanship'" (Pope 1981, 62).[7] The emphasis on psychology supported his theory that accidents were caused primarily by the "unsafe acts" of employees. The minimization of technical fault supported the concept of the culpability of the injured person in accident compensation cases (Hale and Glendon 1987, 31). The techniques for health and safety management advocated by Heinrich in 1931 are evident today in health and safety programs and systems. Techniques for safety management proposed by Heinrich include:

- close supervision

- safety rules

- employee education through training

- posters and films

- hazard identification through analysis of past experience

- survey and inspection

- accident investigation

- job analysis

- methods safety analysis

- production of accident analysis sheets

- approval processes for new construction

- installation of new equipment and changes in work procedures or processes

- establishment of safety committees

- arrangements for emergency and first aid

Heinrich presented lost-time injury frequency rates as the best available measure of effectiveness, complete with the qualification of statistical limitations still common today. Also reminiscent of current approaches is the parallel drawn between the controls in safety and the control of the quality, cost, and quantity of production. The causes of accidents and production faults Heinrich viewed as similar and the control methods as equivalent. Safety, he argued, should be managed like any other business function.

Heinrich's theories of accident causation similarly have continued impact. Perhaps the most enduring legacy of Heinrich is the dichotomy between "unsafe acts" and "unsafe conditions," or the influence of unsafe behavior versus hazards/technical deficiencies as the cause of accidents. At the heart of Heinrich's prevention philosophy was the axiom that the unsafe acts of persons are responsible for a majority of accidents. The axiom was central to Heinrich's domino model of accident causation, which depicted five dominoes ready to fall in sequence, portraying five interconnected factors in an accident sequence. Unsafe acts/conditions were placed in the central position, preceded by inherited or acquired personal faults, and followed by an accident and injury. The removal of the unsafe act/condition was expected to interrupt the sequence. The expected result was prevention of the accident and possible injury. Control of the individual behavior of employees was the key.

Petersen another proponent of the behavioral approach, views the traditional legislative emphasis on physical hazards and technical controls as curtailing the opportunities to develop the behaviorist perspective in the United States. He believes the stage was set for the introduction of a "psychology of safety management era," which would extend Heinrich's principles into new methods for influencing the behavior of people, but the initiative was delayed by the introduction of the Occupational Safety and Health Act of 1970, which he terms the "OSHA era." Petersen comments disparagingly on the resulting emphasis on legislated management responsibility to control physical working conditions and the new focus on compliance with legislation and documentation for government inspection. He deplores the withdrawal of emphasis on people control.[8]

Basic organizational behavior analysis is what is used to identify the actions that put the associate in the risk position. Organizational behavior analysis has been done for a hundred years. Directing the applied research to an organizational application specifically to safety has been going on for around twenty years. Heinrich published work describing the results that he derived by evaluating the accidents from an extensive database compiled by the insurance industry. He came to the conclusion that roughly 90 percent of all incidents are caused by human error. This conclusion became the foundation of what BBS has come to be today. BSS addresses the fact that there are additional reasons for injuries in the workplace—environment, equipment, procedures, and attitudes. Dr. E. Scott Geller of Safety Performance Solutions coined the phrase "behavior-based safety" (BSS) in 1979. It then became the catchphrase of the safety systems industry.[9]

Traditionally, BBS has been used in industrial settings. A new generation has found success using BBS in office/lab settings as well. More recent work has also applied this to the methicillin resistant staphylococcus aureus (MRSA) outbreak in acute intensive care wards in hospitals.

Dr. Luis López-Mena, professor of Work Psychology at the University of Chile, has developed a BBS system—the PTAS method (Psychological Techniques Applied to Safety). The PTAS method has five steps:

- Identify target behavior

- Behavior measurement

- Functional analysis

- Intervention

- Evaluation and follow-up[10]

Criticisms of Behavioral Approaches

Donald J. Eckenfelder has stated that he felt "BBS has virtues but lasted too long and cost too much." He felt that it has been used incorrectly, turning the process into a hindrance instead of help. His analogy was "Water is essential to life: if we fill our lungs with it, it becomes poison."[11]

Some think that BBS has outlived its usefulness. In fact, some feel that BBS "isolates safety instead of integrating it." (But no examples were given.) It is felt that the continuous inspection is not causing attitude or behavior shift and once it is discontinued, all bad habits come back.[12]

Is a Behavioral Approach Right for Your Management System?

As noted, it is not the intention of the authors to make a case for or against the behavioral approach as an element of the integrated management system. Suffice it to say that there are countless others who can profile very well the pros and cons of the behavioral approach. At the end of the day, the determination as to whether the behavioral approach to safety, environmental management, or quality management holds any value to your integrated management system will be determined by your reasoned and intelligent analysis of the approach and whether it is right, and in what configuration, for your business. However, for those looking for a very cogent and reasoned analysis of behavior-based safety and a view of its relationship to your management system, our colleague, Tom Smith of Mocol, Inc., offers some serious food for thought.

What's Wrong with Behavior-Based Safety?

It is not at all unusual these days to pick up a copy of any current safety magazine and find articles and advertisements celebrating the principles, methods, and application of behavior-based safety. There are obviously a large number of advocates of behavior-based safety. Indeed, the only thing that seems to be larger than the number of BBS advocates is the number of articles and advertisements in print.

There comes a time when an idea is so prevalent it is accepted and applied without question. When this happens we are so conditioned to the correctness of it we fail to examine its basic premise. I believe we are at that point when it comes to behavior-based safety. At the risk of invoking the wrath of those safety professionals who advocate its use, I am going to suggest it's time to reexamine the behavior-based safety (BBS) model. I will also propose that in the present and future workplace, BBS is not just partially, but a totally, wrong solution to preventing accidents at work.

The Behavior-Based Safety Model

First, let's examine the basic theory advocated by the behavior-based proponents. The goal of behavior-based safety is to change the behavior of employees from "at-risk" behaviors to "safe" behaviors. They use what is called the ABC model to change human behavior. Most of today's behavioral safety efforts are based on this theory that says all behaviors are a result of antecedents and consequences. This theory, promoted by B. F. Skinner, is that antecedents serve as triggers to observable behaviors. Consequences either enforce or discourage repetition of the behaviors.

The basic behavior-based process consists of identifying observable safe behaviors upstream in the process. Then you need to identify the antecedents (activators) that encourage these safe behaviors and promote them. You should also identify those antecedents that discourage safe behaviors and remove them. Behaviorist theory says those consequences (reinforcement) that are positive, immediate, and certain (rewards) will keep employees working safely. Negative consequences, which are immediate and certain (punishment), discourage unsafe behaviors. The goal for management is to set up a system to control the antecedents and consequences so workers will increase their safe behaviors. The theory being that by setting up a system of well-planned antecedents and consequences, you can control the unsafe behaviors of employees, thus accidents and injuries will be reduced.[13]

Furthermore, the behaviorists believe that consequences are the driving force to changing people's behavior. The tools of positive and negative reinforcement are what are needed to make people behave in the prescribed manner. Consequences are those events that occur as a result of behavior. Positive reinforcement rewards a person for behaving in a certain way. Negative reinforcement provides unwanted or unpleasant consequences. The theory is punishment decreases the probability a behavior will be repeated. Some behaviorists believe that negative reinforcement prompts only a minimal level of compliance. However, positive reinforcement encourages employees to exceed the minimum.

What's in a Theory?

At this point I think we should review the concept of theories. To start with, all theories are correct. Some are just more useful than others. The fact is you can never really prove a theory. You can test it to see if it is valid. The more times the theory works the more confidence you have in it. However, no number of examples proves the theory. The next test of the theory could provide an exception. If there is one exception to your theory, you must either abandon or adjust it so it you can explain and account for the exception.

The Psychological Theory of Behaviorism

The behavior-based safety depends on the psychological theory of behaviorism. This theory explains all human behavior as being driven by external consequences.

B. F. Skinner was one of the most famous psychologists of all time, and he contributed to the concept of operant conditioning (shaping the behavior of an organism using positive and negative reinforcement) as an explanation of why people behave the way they do. His concept of reinforcers as a learning technique developed into "programmed learning."

What Does the Research on Behaviorism Reveal?

Many of the articles that defend and advocate behavior-based safety point out the enormous amount of research substantiating it. They do not mention the large amount of scientific research that refutes it. A major problem with behavior-based safety is the fact that when behaviorism was held up to the scrutiny of the scientific method, it failed.

As behavior research accumulated, it was apparent to even the most ardent followers of the theory that the animals being studied frequently acted in ways the theory couldn't explain.[14]

One major problem was that different animals failed to conform to supposedly universal principles of conditioning. Skinner said, "Pigeon, rat, monkey, which is which? It doesn't matter," but it did matter. The researchers found they could easily train a pigeon to peck at a disc for food, but it was next to impossible to get it to flap its wings for the same reward. They could also get rats to press a bar for food but to get a cat to do it was quite a different matter. There were just too many comparable findings in their research that forced behaviorists to admit that each species had its own built-in processes that made it learn some things easier than others and some things not at all. Their own research showed the laws of learning could not be applied universally.

Behaviorism denies internal processing that goes on in human beings. The behaviorist research could not explain, for example, the behavior in rats when at the beginning of an extinction trial an animal would respond to the stimulus with more vigor than it had during a long series of reinforcements. If a rat that had been getting a food pellet each time it pressed a bar was deprived of the pellet, it would press the bar with more force repetitively. The strict behaviorist theory predicted that the absence of the reward should have weakened the response, not strengthened it.

Behaviorism failed other tests of scientific method. For instance, it could not provide an adequate explanation of memory. Reward and repetition provided only a partial explanation of rat behavior and an even less satisfactory one for human behavior. The internal workings of the mind were more or less ignored by behaviorists and explained away as insignificant. Their use of the stimulus-response bond, for example, did not account for memory and how it works. Even the behaviorist realized that memory was more than a chain of mathematical terms. Memory has different forms, such as short-term and long-term, that behaviorism could not address.

There were many other things that psychologists needed to explore, such as motivation, perception, creativity, problem-solving, experience, and interpersonal relations. Eventually, new data was gathered on these subjects and raised questions that behaviorism couldn't explain. This brought about a paradigm shift and led the way to a new theory of psychology, known as "cognitive science," in the 1960s.

The field of psychology may have advanced beyond behaviorism, but in the field of management, it is quite a different story. Behaviorism is still applied with a vengeance by managers. The fact is it is very useful in a command and control management system. We have applied it with such force and magnitude we now accept its premise without question. Behavior-based safety is a perfect example of this blanket application of behaviorism to the workers.

From the start, behaviorism tried to make use of positive reinforcement as the tool to shape workers' behavior. Obviously, it would not have been a very good idea to stress negative reinforcement as the tool. (No doubt behaviorism would not have enjoyed the acceptance it has if negative reinforcement was its method of choice.)

However, if you examine it carefully you soon realize that positive and negative reinforcement are different sides of the same coin. And that coin doesn't buy much that's worthwhile for motivating people. Both are really saying to employees, do this and you'll get that. In the case of BBS the consequence is positive reinforcement handed out by managers or peers. In actuality the purpose of the reward or punishment is to control or manipulate the behavior of the employee. All this takes place while management ignores or doesn't comprehend the real reason safety problems exist.

Research has shown that positive reinforcement does very little to alter the attitudes that underlie behaviors. You may get a short-term change, but over time employees come to realize they are being manipulated while the safety system stays the same. Using positive reinforcement, no matter what the intentions are by the person administering it, can and does cause resentment between management and the workers. A bad situation is only made worse when workers realize management is ignoring real safety issues while trying to appease employees by getting them to change their behavior using positive reinforcement—carrots or bribes.

Let's look at just a few of the problems with the positive reinforcement approach. There is a basic assumption that positive reinforcement is an enjoyable and greatly appreciated consequence handed out by management. It is believed passing out positive reinforcement will change the at-risk behavior and replace it with one that is safe; therefore, no possible harm could result from its use. Hence, we should use it to motivate workers to do a good job or to work safely. This sounds good, but it has some real drawbacks.

Research has shown using rewards to get people to do what you want them to are not such a clear-cut solution to the question of "How do you change people's behavior?" As early as the 1960s, research projects revealed that rewards (positive reinforcement) were not all that effective when used to try to improve skills or work performance. Some examples are as follows:

1. A researcher asked 128 undergraduates to solve a problem in a lab setting. They were given matches, thumbtacks, and the boxes they came in and asked to mount a candle on a wall using only these materials. Some students were offered $5 to $20 if they succeeded; others weren't promised anything. Those who were working for the financial incentive took 50 percent longer to solve the problem.

2. In another project a researcher asked undergraduates to "select a pattern on each page that was least like the two other patterns on that page." The students "who were not offered money performed significantly better than those who were paid."

Obviously, these two simple examples aren't enough to negate the system of behavior-based safety. But they expose a major flaw in the theory that people in general will do what you want if you use the tool of positive reinforcement. In fact, it can have just the opposite effect.

I invite all proponents of behavior-based safety to do their own research on the psychology of behaviorism as they staunchly advocate in their writings. You will find an enormous amount of research refuting the behaviorist ABC theory. Their first step should be to read the research on the other side of the coin, such as Alfie Kohn's thoroughly researched book, *Punished by Rewards*.[15]

The Basic Problem with the BBS Approach

The cornerstone of behavior-based safety is the principle that the majority of work-related accidents are caused by the unsafe actions of the workers. The traditional safety management theory (developed by Heinrich with no real scientific proof) is you should focus on unsafe actions since they are believed to be the majority (85 to 95 percent) of the reason accidents occur. If you accept this premise, then it is just a small step to the assumption that to improve safety you must concentrate on changing the behavior of the worker.

The fact is accidents are like most bacteria. They are all around us, and most aren't harmful. You can be involved in many kinds of accidents, and there is no real harm. For example, you pick up your clothes from the dry cleaners and find the button you requested to be replaced is still missing. This is an accident, but there is really no harm done. You mention it to the manager, and he blames it on the lazy workers who did not follow instructions. He says he will follow-up with the worker to make certain it doesn't happen the next time. But is this the worker's fault? Or are there other things that could have affected why the task wasn't performed? The basic assumption on the manager's part is someone messed up and making him or her pay is the proper corrective action.

American managers held a similar simplistic view about quality problems in the 1970s and 1980s. Their lament was if only employees would follow management's specifications, the products workers made would have no defects, scraps, rework, or production problems. They really believed all that was necessary to achieve high quality was for the workers to "do it right the first time." This same logic is applied when using behavior-based safety. Since accidents/incidents are caused by unsafe actions on the part of the worker, the key to preventing accidents is to change their "at-risk behavior."

Using this logic, behavior-based safety misses the mark much the same as managers did for quality in the 1970s. A quality management system requires action on the system by management, not the workers, to solve quality problems.

Quality management knows that the problems of output from the system are built into it. You cannot achieve more quality than what the system was designed to deliver. This is also true for safety. The individual worker does not create most quality and safety problems. If your goal is to reduce defects and improve quality, blaming the worker for problems built into the system will not get you any improvement. If you want to improve the outcomes of a system, you must focus on how you manage the system. Enormous gains have been made to reduce the defects, scrap, and rework inherent in work systems using quality management theories.

What Does Cause Accidents?

A basic shift is necessary in your understanding of why things go wrong that leads to accidents, scrap, rework, and defects in a work system. New knowledge of why accidents/incidents happen must be applied. In a quality management system, managers understand accidents result from common causes and special causes. Common causes are faults in the elements of a system. Special causes are causes that are unusual and not normally found in the system. They can come and go without any warning. In a quality management system, common causes account for 85 to 95 percent of your problems and special causes are responsible for the remaining 5 to 15 percent. This is the theory of what causes accidents in a quality management system. It is much more useful as it will help everyone understand how to fix the system instead of fixing the blame for accidents.

This requires a major shift in the accident causation model. The simple explanation that unsafe actions and unsafe conditions cause accidents will not suffice. The quality theory again can be used to provide a much better understanding of why accidents happen at work. Quality theory has taught us that defects, mistakes, scrap, and rework are caused by the way we manage the work system, not the miscues of the workers. This same knowledge must be applied in safety. Accidents are caused by how we manage the work system.

The Power Shift

Quality systems created a major shift in how companies manage their work processes. W. Edwards Deming taught us all work is a system, and a system has to be managed. (He would often say the shouting slogans or putting up posters encouraging workers to "do it right the first time" or "safety is your [the employee's] job" were a waste of time.) Companies have learned that in order to improve productivity and customer satisfaction they must improve quality—period. Improving quality requires a new management theory. Until recently, the management system of choice was to manage for quantity using the command and control model. In today's world managing for quantity will not succeed.

Quantity methods used from the 1950s to the 1970s relied on building the product, inspecting it, and selling it. Companies were more concerned with production than quality. They could sell anything they made. Now they are faced with the reality that competition may come from anywhere in the world. To compete, their products and services must have value and lower costs than their competitors. They must also anticipate the needs of their customers and fulfill these needs even though the customer often doesn't know what they want.

Quality management methods also require the "voice of the customers" be integrated into your system. If you don't do this, your competitors will and you will lose customers. To understand and incorporate the voice of the customer in your system, you have to continually research their needs and reinvent products and services to meet these needs. Customers are people who benefit from your product and service.

In the command and control method there is a division of labor. Managers do all the thinking, and workers do the work. They just punch in, catch hell, and punch out. Good parts are separated from the bad by inspecting them at the end of the production line. They are reworked or scraped. Emphasis is placed on inspections to achieve quality. Catch the bad stuff and ship the good stuff. This is a very inefficient way to make things, but it worked and it paid off handsomely.

Quality Management Systems

In the 1970s a quality revolution was started in the United States by the import of products from Japan. This included, but was not limited to, products previously manufactured in the United States (television sets, radios, calculators, and automobiles). This revolution focused on how to manage a work system to improve quality instead of concentrating on mass quantity as the goal.

The revolutionary idea in this management system is everyone who works in the system is needed to study the problems in it and then make improvements. The goal of this system is to reduce waste, scrap, rework, and accidents so you can make good products. In this system workers are hired for their mental labor as well as their manual labor. It does not require command and control of the workers. The goal is to get control of the system. Control is not the goal but the effect of good management.

In a quality management system the mental labor of all employees is needed to fix the system. Everyone must learn the tools to identify system problems and take the proper action to fix the system instead of fixing the blame. (Fixing the blame is very costly and destroys teamwork.) In this work setting the role of managers is changed. Workers "on the line" now learn how to record data about their processes. They work in teams instead of for the boss. In some companies there is no boss. The teams study their operations and look for better ways to do the job, eliminate waste, scrap, and rework before it happens—not after. In short, teams replace the old frontline supervisor whose job it was to make workers do their jobs correctly.

This management system is slowly evolving. The new model of how we will manage in the twenty-first century is not complete and will probably continue to evolve over the next decade. One thing for certain, it will not look anything like the command and control model we have used and are presently dismantling.

The point is all workers' roles change in a quality management system. In the command and control model, the line workers' ideas, creativity, and motivation were not required. Management took care of these things. The new management model will require that everyone's ideas, creativity, ingenuity, and motivation are paramount to the success of the organization.

Problems for BBS in the New Quality Management System

We seem to be moving away from the roots of behaviorism in the new quality management models being used by companies. The following are just some of the problems the BBS model creates when applied to the new quality management system:

- A major problem for behavior-based safety is it requires and relies on external motivators (antecedents and consequences) to change people's behavior. As explained earlier, these techniques did not work all that well on rats and other animals, let alone human beings. The reality is they are more likely to be de-motivators in the new quality management system described above. Studies have shown that the largest factors to cause dissatisfaction on the job are "company policy and administration."[16] These are the very things BBS tries to enforce when trying to change employee behaviors.

- The next problem for behavior-based safety is that extrinsic motivators destroy the intrinsic motivation that is inherent in people to do good work and work safely. The antecedent-behavior-consequences model assumes an extrinsic motivator is required to make the employee behave a certain way. I have yet to meet an employee that sets out in the morning with a goal of trying to get injured on the job. Yet the basic premise of behavior-based safety is employees need to be motivated to exercise "safe behaviors." A system of reinforcement and incentives is applied to accomplish this motivational goal. The reinforcement ranges from the negative (reprimands) to the positive (rewards, compliments, bribes) with the goal of having the individual see the error of his ways and then changing the at-risk behavior so accidents will be avoided. (It also begs the question, if behaviorism works so well for safety, why isn't it used in the quality arena? All one has to do is read any serious work on quality by any of the quality gurus and you will realize that the workers weren't responsible for quality problems—it was management.)

- As mentioned earlier there is a large body of research that contradicts the widely held, common-sense belief that carrots and sticks will result in a permanent attitudinal change. Research has shown positive reinforcement, no matter what form it is administered by BBS methods, will only provide a temporary change. There is even a greater danger due to the fact that a short-term success will result in a perception that the real safety problem has been solved. In the long run, positive reinforcement may cause more harm than good. When workers eventually have to face the safety problems after their heroic efforts to avoid an injury are defeated by the hazards built into the system, an ever-deeper chasm is created between them and management.

- There is little thought given to another problem with behavior-based safety. That is the managers who use it look upon employees only as suppliers of manual labor in the production system. One behaviorist points out companies are only renting the behavior of the employee. Therefore, all that is required by management is to control the behavior through the use of positive and negative reinforcement. It is the major conceit of command and control managers that they must motivate the workers since they are not already motivated to do a good job or control their own unsafe actions.[17]

- The problem is in a quality management system, employees are both a customer and a supplier in the work system. If safety management is going to achieve the awesome levels of improvement seen in quality, it will have to treat workers as customers first and suppliers second. If you look at safety as a system used to manage the work system, you must first examine, who are the people that will benefit from the activities and processes of safety? The obvious answer is the workers doing the work. They are the first customers of safety management and should be handled as you would any customer.

- To satisfy customers, you must answer the following questions: Who are your customers? What do they want and need? How do you know they are satisfied? The BBS model pays no attention to this exercise. Indeed, the workers are treated as though they don't know anything about what they want or need when it comes to safety. They should just do what they're told and accept the safety situation as it is. The best employees are ones who comply with the prescribed methods already designed by management. In the world of quality the customer defines quality. The same is true for safety. Since employees know the job and hazards associated with it better than anyone else, they should be the ones telling safety management about the problems with the methods. Now some will think I'm advocating the inmates should take control of the asylum. This is not at all what I'm saying. Workers will gladly help management when it comes to making the job safer. Given the opportunity, they often provide solutions less costly than the injuries built into the system. Ergonomic problems come to mind immediately, but other less-obvious safety problems are equally attacked and results attained.

- Another problem with behavior-based safety is the assumption there is one "safe" way to do the job and it can be applied to all workers. BBS assumes you can observe the employee's behaviors, compare them to the prescribed safe behavior, and correct the employee's at-risk behavior using activators and consequences. This means the "at-risk behavior" must be changed. No thought or attempt is made to get any input into whether or not the worker, the main safety customer, defines the job as "safe."

This approach is in direct conflict with the theory of a quality system in which the employees are given much more respect. The individual employee knows more about the issues of quality than management because they are closest to the job. That is why quality management systems make use of operational definitions. Workers control the process and must have a voice in what specifications mean. The only way a specification can have real meaning is to develop an operational definition. When the BBS observation teams pass judgment on the workers being observed, they typically use safety specifications provided by nonelective suppliers such as OSHA, consultants, or management-created job safety analysis. What does "at-risk behavior" mean? At risk because it doesn't meet OSHA regulations? or corporate job safety analysis? or for the comfort of the worker doing the job? Each one of these definitions would be different and produce different results. Without an operational definition of what is "safe," a safety specification is meaningless.

In the past, if a quality problem existed, management was prone to blame the workers for not following safety instructions. This mistake is repeated in behavior-based safety. The fact is, the workers know more about safety problems on the job than anyone else in the system. They do not create them. Most safety problems are built into work systems, and it will take action by management with the help of the workers to reduce or eliminate them.

- The BBS approach sees cooperation as workers meeting the instructions for safety created by management and regulators. Cooperation, therefore, equals compliance by the workers with prescribed management activities. That is not the type of cooperation we are talking about. Cooperation desired in a quality management system is to have management and hourly people work together to change the system so it meets the needs of both external and internal customers. I think everyone has experienced the anxiety and confusion of having someone watch you to see if you are doing your job properly. It's not a very pleasant way to learn, and the long-term consequences are usually negative. First, the anxiety created from the process can be really upsetting to the person being monitored. Second, it perpetuates the myth that people must be managed or they will mess up.

- And finally, the BBS process is what the Japanese call a form of "muda"—waste. Paying supervision and peers to watch others work and then applying an outmoded theory to the outcome is wasteful and contradicts continual improvement methods.[18] Focusing on the unsafe actions of the individual has nothing to do with the real upstream factors that create them—the command and control methods prevalent in the BBS management system. Managers who truly understand quality management systems have much better ways of spending their time, mainly studying, improving, and fixing the safety system with the help of the workers. Not by asking them to comply with safety rules, but by setting up a system in which their critical thinking can be applied to their work environment to change the system.

Systems Thinking Applied to Safety

The way in which employees are interviewed, trained, treated by management on the job, the design of work methods, materials, machinery, and equipment (the system) have a great deal more to do with why accidents happen at work than "unsafe actions." The simple idea that unsafe actions by workers are the driving force that create incidents and accidents is now outdated. This technique of focusing on the event (the unsafe action) in the hope that it will lead to understanding why it happened is doomed to failure. The reality is, the system creates the behavior of both managers and workers. We know you can replace an entire workforce with new people and they will produce the same results. This is true for quality and safety. Systems can be very complex. It is the complexity and variation inherent in all components of the system that generate the defects, scrap, rework, incidents, and accidents.[19]

When you attain the knowledge that the system itself causes accidents, BBS is no longer useful. It is even detrimental because workers have already learned about quality management techniques. You create a situation of organizational schizophrenia. On one hand management freely engages and accepts the assistance of line workers to study and improve quality in their work systems. On the other hand, management enlists behaviorist principles to manipulate employees' actions instead of using quality management methods to fix safety problems built into the work system. Employees now know and understand systems thinking. They've applied it in quality. Once you've learned a new and better way of doing something, you aren't going back to the inferior system.

The key is to apply systems thinking to safety management. With quality systems we learned that work is a system. A system is a series of events that must have an aim. When you know the aim of the system, everyone must work together in a cooperative manner to achieve the aim. Businesses must have an aim of satisfying and taking care of the customer. If you don't, someone else will, and you will lose business. This principle must be applied in safety management.

How you manage a system is a system in itself. I've described earlier the command and control system. Behavior-based safety fits well with this model. It does not fit at all with a quality management model. The reason being is the employees are considered both customers and then suppliers in the quality system. It is true employees do get paid to do their jobs. However, in a quality management system, work previously reserved for managers is now assigned to line employees. They solve problems of quality on the line. They have the authority to make changes and spend money to improve the system. This changes everything. Workers are required to think on the job. They can come up with solutions using their own ideas about what should be changed to improve quality and productivity. BBS all but eliminates any intrinsic motivation employees have, and for this reason, it will fail in the new quality management systems. When it comes to how you manage a work system, what is true for quality is also true for safety. For the reasons pointed out in this article, I believe quality management systems, not behavior-based safety, will drive the new safety management model we will be using in the twenty-first century and beyond.

PROFOUND THINKING: MANAGEMENT SYSTEMS—THE DEMING WAY: A LESSON FOR ALL INTEGRATED MANAGEMENT SYSTEM PRACTITIONERS

It's been suggested in popular literature and articles that one of the main reasons conventional approaches to safety management systems (sometimes called safety programs) didn't work was because they were predicated on old management theories that didn't tap into the intellectual capabilities of the workforce who were supposedly contributing so much to the productivity and quality of goods and services being provided by the organization. With the shrinking of global markets and increased competition between countries for valuable market share of a global economy, it was becoming increasingly obvious to those who owned the means of production that if they were to compete on a global scale, more resources would have to be brought to the table—and those resources were renewable and already available—mental as well as manual labor.

Beginning in the mid-1970s, many in the safety profession were starting to look outside their industry-based borders and were increasingly looking to a movement known as TQM (total quality management). While this movement would later become very popular through the standards of ISO 9000 and 14000 series, there were a number of pioneers who were viewed by many as the new gurus of quality, and many in the safety profession copied their approaches while putting a unique safety spin on their approach.

One of those quality pioneers who many practitioners related to was Edwards Deming, author of a number of books on quality, productivity, and competition. While there are many different theories about how to create an effective management system, Deming's concept of a fourteen-point "formula" for effectively getting America into a more competitive mind-set was music to the ears of many management systems advocates, as it offered a road map of sorts by which quality (or safety) could be set to a logical, if somewhat common sense, road map. It's clear that when you read Deming's fourteen points there is some sort of light bulb that clicks on inside one's head, and a moment of clarity results.

Deming's Fourteen Points

Deming offered fourteen key principles for management for transforming business effectiveness. The points were first presented in his book *Out of the Crisis*.

- Create constancy of purpose toward improvement of product and service, with the aim to become competitive and stay in business and to provide jobs.

- Adopt the new philosophy. We are in a new economic age. Western management must awaken to the challenge, must learn their responsibilities, and take on leadership for change.

- Cease dependence on inspection to achieve quality. Eliminate the need for inspection on a mass basis by building quality into the product in the first place.

- End the practice of awarding business on the basis of price tag. Instead, minimize total cost. Move toward a single supplier for any one item, on a long-term relationship of loyalty and trust.

- Improve constantly and forever the system of production and service to improve quality and productivity, and thus constantly decrease cost.

- Institute training on the job.

- Institute leadership. The aim of supervision should be to help people and machines and gadgets to do a better job. Supervision of management is in need of overhaul, as well as supervision of production workers.

- Drive out fear, so that everyone may work effectively for the company.

- Break down barriers between departments. People in research, design, sales, and production must work as a team to foresee problems of production and in use that may be encountered with the product or service.

- Eliminate slogans, exhortations, and targets for the workforce asking for zero defects and new levels of productivity. Such exhortations only create adversarial relationships, as the bulk of the causes of low quality and low productivity belong to the system and thus lie beyond the power of the workforce.

    a. Eliminate work standards (quotas) on the factory floor. Substitute leadership.

b. Eliminate management by objective. Eliminate management by numbers, numerical goals. Substitute leadership.

c. Remove barriers that rob the hourly worker of his or her right to pride of workmanship. The responsibility of supervisors must be changed from sheer numbers to quality.

d. Remove barriers that rob people in management and in engineering of their right to pride of workmanship. This means, inter alia, abolishment of the annual or merit rating and of management by objective.

- Institute a vigorous program of education and self-improvement.

- Put everybody in the company to work to accomplish the transformation. The transformation is everybody's work.[1]

Quality Management and a "New Loss Control Management Theory"

In a July/August article by Thomas A. Smith titled "A New Loss Control Management Theory," Smith proposed an approach to safety management obviously patterned on Deming's fourteen points for an effective management system. For those looking for a cogent, yet practical, blueprint upon which to hang their hat, a reasonable approach for helping guide the focus of an integrated management system, Smith offers the following (any reference to the word *safety* can also include quality and environment).

1. Create a constancy of purpose to improve all safety efforts in all company operations—accidents are the same as producing scrap. They are a failure of the management system to perform its ultimate responsibility: to perpetuate the company as a viable and healthy entity. The cost of accidents is devastating to a company's economic health. Management can no longer blame employees for accident frequencies. The management team designs the system in which employees participate. So if accidents are occurring, management must own up to the fact it is responsible. This must be done to increase the competitiveness of the company since accidents take too much away from the company both in human and economic terms. Companies are not in the business to manufacture scrap. Accidents are the most obvious manifestation of lack of quality and of modern management's confusion about its role.

2. Adopt a new loss control philosophy. There are new competitive pressures to improve efficiencies of all operations. Accidents are the same as producing scrap. We can no longer live with commonly accepted levels of delays, mistakes, defective equipment, and work habits. Management must constantly work to improve the work system for employees.

3. Find problems—under the old theory, managers set up the system, implemented it, and watched it churn out the product or service. As things moved along there were problems, but they were "taken care of" later. This is the point at which managers would criticize employee attitude and behavior, but attitudes and behaviors are very abstract concepts. The problems created by management were easily pawned off on employees. Yet this is what managers say most often when asked why their company is having problems with safety. In fact, the managers are usually responsible for the attitudes and behaviors of their workforce.

4. Institute methods of team decision-making and problem-solving on the job, so that all employees work on and solve problems. If you don't tap the mental labor of your workforce, your company will be penalized out of existence.

5. Institute modern methods of supervision for all workers. The responsibility of the foreperson must be changed from sheer numbers to facilitators of the safety effort.

6. Management must respond immediately to reports from supervisors about barriers to safety. When management is really concerned about the company's competitiveness, it should respond to issues raised by employees on problems with the safety effort. This type of feedback shouldn't be considered negative but should be viewed as opportunities to make operations safer, more productive, and therefore hopefully increase product or service quality as well as employee morale and safety.

7. Drive out fear so that everyone can work effectively. Historically, the use of fear by management has been seen as a very powerful motivator; however, it's been suggested that managers who use overt methods of intimidation and fear are often resented by workers. This resentment can be very destructive to any organization.

8. Break down barriers between departments. We all work for the same company, and our competitiveness is enhanced when the synergy of all groups is designed to work in unison. When barriers are broken down,

employees can feel safe in addressing unsafe conditions or other scenarios that could lead to accidents, without fear of reprisal.

9. Allow employees to set their own goals for safety. Management objectives expressed in things like numerical targets, posters, and safety slogans never worked, and they never made anyone work more safely. This will require perhaps the most dramatic deviation from those ideals that most management holds most dear. Most managers get assessed and evaluated on how well they are meeting their objectives, targets, or key performance indicators. Giving workers responsibility may seem like a manager abdicating his or her responsibility. Some would ask, "If managers don't have defined goals and objectives, how will the company succeed?" How, indeed. But when it comes to setting safety management system objectives, a little abdication and anointing of workers as keepers of select safety management system objectives can do wonders for employee ownership of safety.

10. Remove any barriers, real or perceived, that prevent workers from working in accordance with acceptable and defined safety standards or any other objective or subjective safety standards that are designed to improve worker or process safety. Typically, management systems have been designed by management and are usually beyond the direct control of workers. So it's been suggested that management should "mentor" those who may not have direct access to those systems, policies, and procedures that determine work, work methods, and processes.

11. Reduce turnover. It's been said that turnover devastates the quality, productivity, and safety efforts of the entire company. Of course, turnover is very often the result of workers seeking to improve their lot in life, and that lot may or may not always be with the same company; however, when it comes to turnover, any barriers that the organization can identify that may be an impediment to effective safety performance should be marginalized. At the end of the day this means that those workers who make a commitment to stay with the employer should be encouraged, as long as they are with that employer, to make whatever contributions they deem necessary to help continuously improve safety performance of the organization.

12. Put in place a robust system of training and education for everyone. As it relates to the concept of continuous improvement, key to the opportunity of taking advantage of continuous improvement opportunities

are initiatives manifested in education and training scenarios. Just be cautioned—this is not a one-time experience. In order to reap the long-term benefits of education and training, be prepared to commit to the long term.

13. Create a structure in top management that will reinforce and emphasize the previously noted twelve points. In other words, say what you do . . . do what you say, and prove it. Then do it over again. It's not attractive or sexy, but it works, and it's practical. Quality must be the main emphasis of any company that intends to compete, and high quality cannot be achieved without a prudent and effective safety management system as well.[2]

A Final Management System Lesson from Deming

Many times those of us in the safety, quality, and environmental management business tend to spend a lot of time on statistics, numbers, concepts, and evidence-based initiatives. But it is sometimes refreshing to take another approach to our management system strategies and apply some good, old-fashioned reasoning and what some would call horse sense to our daily grind. That's why there is some cause for reflection in some of the sayings Deming hung his hat on, and while we don't offer them here as window dressing, they are offered as an opportunity to consider them within the context of how each and every one of us manage the strategic implementation of our management systems on a day-to-day basis.

- "What is a system? A system is a network of interdependent components that work together to try to accomplish the aim of the system. A system must have an aim. Without an aim, there is no system. The aim of the system must be clear to everyone in the system. The aim must include plans for the future. The aim is a value judgment. (We are of course talking here about a man-made system.)"

- "A system must be managed. It will not manage itself. Left to themselves in the Western world, components become selfish, competitive. We can not afford the destructive effect of competition."

- "To successfully respond to the myriad of changes that shake the world, transformation into a new style of management is required. The route to take is what I call profound knowledge—knowledge for leadership of transformation."

- "The worker is not the problem. The problem is at the top! Management! Management's job. It is management's job to direct the efforts of all components toward the aim of the system. The first step is clarification: everyone in the organization must understand the aim of the system, and how to direct his efforts toward it. Everyone must understand the damage and loss to the whole organization from a team that seeks to become a selfish, independent, profit center."[3]

Perhaps it's time to reconsider our approach on overmanaging people and undermanaging our management systems.

INTEGRATED MANAGEMENT SYSTEMS ROI: THE COST-BENEFIT PROPOSITION FOR INTEGRATED MANAGEMENT SYSTEMS

There have been many theories proposed with respect to how best to "market" the positive aspects of a strategic and rationalized approach to management systems. There have been volumes written on the legal, moral, ethical, and financial benefits of an effective occupational health and safety management system, for example.

While there has been considerable debate on which approach is most prudent or advisable for selling organizations and their leadership, for those wishing to link the cost-benefit between safety and quality, there is evidence that can be referenced.

While laws and regulations may establish what many refer to as the "minimum" requirements for safety, in some jurisdictions, doing less or only what the law requires may expose an organization to the risk of liability. In jurisdictions where the standard of care can be dependent on the risks associated with an enterprise, doing the minimum may not be enough.

Impact on Financial Performance—ISO

It's no secret that the investment in time, energy, and resources to have an effective occupational health and safety management system can be great. But what is the real cost and ROI? Is there any evidence that an occupational health and safety management system, or an integrated management system, is worth the effort? While there is not a lot of published evidence available, there are some studies that should be referenced by those seeking to rationalize their integrated management system.

In a study conducted by Rodney McAdam, the experiences of select small businesses in Northern Ireland with under a hundred employees indicated companies registered to ISO 9000 series standards were up to five times more likely to experience select benefits than those small businesses not having any relationship with ISO 9000. Additionally, three other studies provided more evidence of the cost-benefit and ROI between ISO and corporate performance.[1]

In a 2002 study by the University of California at Los Angeles, a study titled "The Financial Impact of ISO 9000 Certification in the U.S.: An Empirical Analysis," the authors looked at a number of publicly traded companies and compared the performance of those who were and were not certified. According to the study's findings, in almost all of the cases, the companies that were registered to ISO demonstrated substantially higher return on assets in the subsequent ten years than the non-ISO registered companies.[2]

Also in a 2002 study, 800 businesses—50 percent of which were registered to ISO 9000—were examined to determine if there was any relationship between sales, profitability, and ISO registration. The study's audits concluded that while there wasn't enough conclusive evidence to demonstrate a direct cause-and-effect relationship between ISO and profitability, the authors did conclude that it was the efforts associated with pursuing certification that might have been the difference in the financial performance of the two study groups. In other words, those companies that have a focus on the positive aspects of certification were more likely to be successful than the companies with no ISO focus.[3]

Finally, a study by Rajan and Tamini in 2003 considered the relationship between ISO registration and benefits to shareholders of public companies. The authors assessed the stock performance of a number of companies—some that were ISO registered compared to some that were not. The result of the study found that those companies that had achieved ISO registration had higher stock-price growth. Specifically, it was determined that for $100k in an investment portfolio of non-ISO registered companies, they would have supposedly been valued at approximately $424k around nine years later; however, that same $100k invested in an ISO registered company, over the same nine-year period, would have been valued at approximately $814k . . . almost double the non-ISO registered company.[4]

So what might we reasonably extrapolate from these findings with respect to a possible relationship to occupational health and safety and environmental management? Granted, the expressed purpose of a quality management approach is to enhance and ensure excellence in product development and customer service. And it is generally agreed that occupational health and safety and environmental management can be said to devote their attention to meeting or exceeding legislative expectations for the prevention of personal injury or harm to the environment. But contemporary approaches to safety and environmental management emphasize value-added and strategic approaches rather than mere compliance to regulations. So, integral to the success of an integrated management system is rationalizing the key elements of the quality safety environmental management equation for maximum return on investment for the business.

So while there may not be as many definitive research models available, they do demonstrate that an occupational health and safety management system is always a financially sound investment, and there is a body of knowledge that gives credence to the fact that an effectively implemented and maintained quality management system can have a positive impact on safety and an environmental management system, if implemented with integrity, intelligence, and strategic thinking.[5] At the end of the day, many of our approaches to management system discipline are very often a variation of whatever model of control we happen to believe in at the time.

CHAPTER NINE
TECHNOLOGY CAN MAKE THE DIFFERENCE: MANAGEMENT SYSTEM TECHNOLOGY SOLUTIONS

The management system practitioners of today have a number of different advantages over colleagues of ten to fifteen years ago. The proliferation of software solutions to take the mundane and drudgery out of management system coordination (documentation control and management, data analysis, root cause/hazard analysis, action tracking, auditing, customer communication) is almost an essential for today's management system practitiner. On second thought, it is essential.

For years, management systems were, and some would argue, still are, characterized by unending volumes of paper records, binders, and documentation. So much so, in fact, that much of the negative about management systems is the perception that they can be nothing more than a massive paper chase. And in some respects, for some organizations, that assertion is correct.

The role of an effective management system should help to add significant value to an organization through the use of timely, accurate, and meaningful information and data. Looking at stacks and stacks of paper piled high on a desk may tell you that you and your colleagues have been doing something, but there may be a gold mine of data in that pile that you can never extract due to the nature of paper-based documentation.

Many management system practitioners are familiar with the continual improvement cycle model: Plan-Do-Check-Act. This model basically follows the guideline of "say what you do, do what you say, and prove it." And while pure conformance to management system requirement is only one aspect of an effective management system, so to is the effective management of information and data.

For some organizations, the decision to build in-house software is rationalized, while many prefer to contract the development of a management system software solution to proven technologies. In looking at technology-based solutions for the management system, the authors are not advocating one approach over another; however, as the authors have had significant experience in designing and building in-house solutions, as well as custom, off-the-shelf management system software solutions, we will profile the pros and cons of both approaches. The objective, however, should be to ensure that whatever route you choose (in-house vs. contracted out, commercial off-the-shelf) you have some confidence at the end of the day that the technology solution you've chosen can add the value to your management system that you and your management team expect. Also, the data you generate from your management system initiatives should generate information to help you and your management team manage better, make better and more informed decisions, and ultimately improve the value of your management systems. Let's take a brief look at some of these management system opportunities that can be further enhanced by some of the leading-edge technology solutions that are on the market.

Documentation Control and Management

As previously noted, one of the complaints against structured management systems is the amount of information and documentation required to maintain the system to a level deemed appropriate by management system practitioners and internal and outside auditors. For most activities associated with your management system, there can be a wide array of policies, practices, and procedures that need to be managed, updated, communicated, and available for ongoing revision and update.

Many in-house and third-party applications currently available on the market use some variation of a data warehouse to enable a document repository for the maintenance and coordination of management system documentation. Using a data warehouse with the ability to store, sort, and manage management system documents provides an easy-to-access site for everyone within the organization. Further security-based access can ensure that only those who have a need to access the documents can do so, and read/write-only access can help protect sensitive data from accidental deletion.

Take ten minutes to run a search on Google and you'll come to quickly realize that many of the third-party applications currently on the market have migrated from old client-based technology solutions to completely web-enabled solutions, whether through a client's own intranet or available through the vendor's website through an ASP web-hosted solutions. The critical issue here is for the integrated management system to be able to be designed in such as way as to make the ease of access for critical documentation readily available in an easy-to-access/read format.

Root Cause/Hazard Analysis

There is no reason why management system practitioners need rely on paper-based models for conducting problem-solving and root cause analysis anymore. The only caution is that you should not become a slave to the functionality of limited features of select software solutions currently on the market. When a software vendor requires you to change your management system approach to meet the limitations of his or her software solution, you know it's time to seek another solution. That is why it's so critically important to ensure your functional requirements for a management system software solution are clearly and thoroughly defined. Making your management system software work to complement your management system is much better than having to consider changing the way you do business because of the limitations of a piece of software. As a word of advice for those without a technical background seeking technical software solutions—if the off-the-shelf solutions you identify do not provide 100 percent of the functionality you require (and many won't) press the vendor to work with you for custom modifications to meet your requirements. Whether you're able to secure these custom modifications as part of your purchase or whether you need to negotiate to help pay or fund the modifications, getting your functional requirements at the end of the day is your ultimate objective.

Confessions of a Vice President of Management System Software

It wasn't all that long ago that one of the authors, Wayne Pardy, was vice president of marketing for Q5 Systems Limited. Q5 is an international leader in software management applications for integrated management systems, with specific emphasis on audit, inspection, and action-tracking software solutions. It was in this role that Pardy got to see the management system business from a different perspective—that of the management system practitioner looking for a technology solution for his or her unique management system structure, while at the same time looking for every modification possible (usually for no cost!) and that was created in the image of the respective culture and administrative requirement of each and every company. And yet while they were all different, they were all the same.

Most management system practitioners have little or no experience in technology solutions for their management system requirements. This is not surprising, but it can be frustrating to both a management system technology vendor, who, while sometimes trying, cannot be all things to all clients. And it can be frustrating to the customer who wonders why "your" software doesn't do what he or she wants it to do. While many software vendors will assume a "take it or leave it" attitude, other management system software vendors are very willing to work with a customer to try, as much as reasonably possible, based on their technology platform and available resources, to work to "customize" the one-size-fits-all technology solution to your respective requirements. For those looking for technology solutions for their integrated management systems, a word of advice from an informed industry insider—make sure you define your functional requirements as clearly and definitively as you can. Don't take the approach of, "when I see it I'll know it." You need to do just as much research on a technology solution as you did in the research and design phase for your integrated management system. Technology solutions are not inexpensive, and like the saying goes, "you get what you pay for." But it is critically important that you not let the vendor define your requirements. You must be crystal-clear on your defined functionality. And you must try to ensure that, though cost is a factor, it should not be the most critical factor. You don't want to get stuck with a moderately priced technology solution that everyone complains about and doesn't provide good information and value.

The more flexible the software, the more you as the user can define select features, fields, and reporting options, and the better the software solution will complement your existing management system.

Action Tracking

The area of corrective and preventive action tracking is one that requires significant due diligence. When consulting with clients, the authors typically ask the question of pending actions, "If this action is never acted upon, would there be a consequence?"

The fundamental premise of this question is to first determine whether there is any value in the action in the first place; however, especially in the safety and environmental management area, the potential legal consequences of not meeting a regulatory oversight could be severe. That is not to say that on the quality front there would not be severe consequences with missing or not addressing identified corrective or preventive actions. What must be acknowledged is that with the ever-increasing liability landscape that exists today, especially in North America, the consequences of not addressing actions stemming from critical safety or environmental issues can be crucial.

When considering a technology solution for your action-tracking requirements, here are some key issues to keep in mind when developing an in-house solution or seeking a third-party application.

- The ability to track any action, stemming from any source.

- The ability to customize the system with "user defined fields." For example, if you plan on tracking actions stemming from investigations, environmental spills, or customer complaints, it would be beneficial to have some way of segregating the status of these respective actions such that required resources can be directed toward where they are needed most.

- The ability to assign various levels of security for creating, modifying, completing, and approving actions. These functions may or may not be conducted by the same individual every time.

- The ability to enable standard and custom reporting for all actions, including those that are coming due and overdue. You should also be able to sort the actions by individual, department, or work group, contractor, etc. In other words, the application should be able to mirror any organizational chart of corporate structure, regardless of how complex.

- Accessibility—web-based access is the standard these days. Carefully consider any option that does not offer web-based access and functionality.

Innovation Leads the Way

The most innovative systems are those that have some mobility feature to enable the workforce to use the technology while out of the office. Q5AIMS, for example, has integrated the field mobility of pocket PC, laptop PC, or tablet PC in order to facilitate field use. Disconnected from the main database, workers can do audits, inspections, and corrective action tracking all in the field, from wherever in the world they are working. A simple username and password entered upon logging back into the main website uploads all the data entered in the field, eliminating at least a couple of steps of manual data entry. So at any time, a corrective action can be initiated, synchronized with the main database upon return to the office, and synergies achieved whereby your management system staff no longer are constrained by having to be in an office and logged on to your network or server.

Audit Management

This is the area in which those management system technologies that have a mobility application win hands down over paper checklists and word-processing software.

The most advances in management system auditing over the past five years haven't necessarily been with system or standards but with technology solutions. The ability to capitalize on a field-enabled audit management system, with integrated action-tracking features, puts those organizations that leverage this technology leaps and bounds ahead of the paper-based, word-processor devotees.

Here's a typical scenario. Take any management system audit you can imagine (checklist-based, open-ended questions, etc.). You design your audit in the software, do your audit in the field, and "synch" it back when you have access to a network connection. Finalize your report, and the audit is finished. But wait. The client wants a copy of the report before your audit team leaves the site. No problem . . . use the print feature on the mobility solution and you can leave a complete audit report with your client without ever having to return to the office.

The drawback with most paper-based audit systems is that the data cannot be mined, sorted, or queried. Many still use word-processing software to prepare the audit report, and while the audit is available for reading, over the course of time (and a multitude of audits) the data amassed from numerous audits doesn't tell you anything. You have to manually sort through all that data and try to manipulate it to identify issues, trends, or problem areas.

If you're looking for a value-added audit technology, look for one that can analyze and tend by sections and actual questions in your audit. This will also satisfy the requirement of some standards that require you to demonstrate analysis of data, and audit data can generate meaningful information about issues and trends.

Customer Communication and Feedback

There are many options available on the market today for management system specialists looking to implement a technology solution to add value to their current management system. We thought we would provide you with a small overview of some of the products that are currently available on the market which, in the opinion of the authors, offer good potential for complementing the strategic approach to management system and system practice.

Authors' Note

The following is not meant to be a complete overview of the many and varied different types of management system software solutions available on the market today. Like most organizations, if you are looking for a software solution to enhance the effectiveness of your management system processes, your first prudent step is a functional requirement assessment of what you want the system to do. Not knowing what functionality you desire from a software solution can have you running in circles. Worse still, functionality will become very subjective, and you'll simply be responding to the sales tactics and spin of software salespersons whose job, rightfully, is to sell software. Whether what they are selling is right for your management system should not be left up to a software salesperson. If the company is as forward-thinking and progressive as they need to be in today's software market, most of the functionality you desire will be available, with the ability to customize in-house. While it is very rare to get 100 percent user-defined functionality in a commercial, off-the-shelf (COTS) software solution, if the solution has been designed by those who know the management system business, you should be at least getting a software solution that will enable you to adapt it to your current business realities. The reference made to these select management system software vendors in no way constitutes an endorsement by the authors of these software vendors. There may be other management system technology available on the market as well. As with any software purchase, always do your homework. A simple query in Google will provide you with plenty of options for consideration.

Some Management System Technology Vendors Worthy of Checking Out

Intelex

Intelex Technologies, Inc. (Intelex) was founded in 1992 to develop and market software systems designed to drive continual improvement in enterprise environmental, quality, and health and safety performance. In early 1999 Intelex began the conversion of the PC-based product line to an entirely new web-based platform. This early adoption of web-based technology proved to be an excellent decision, enabling Intelex to release its first 100 percent web-based system in the summer of 2000.

Intelex has continued its commitment to continual improvement by adding to and enhancing the Intelex web-based system. Intelex now offers a library of over fifty unique modules available to be seamlessly integrated into the Intelex platform. Each module has been carefully crafted and designed to address a specific business need, enabling organizations to pick and choose the solutions right for them.

Intelex offers configurable business performance management solutions that enable organizations to roll up their key performance indicators to all levels of the organization by way of a user-friendly, configurable, graphical dashboard. The Intelex key performance indicators (iKPI) module enables custom data points, forms, routings, and tiered calculations to be developed. All of these pieces can then be assembled into form-triggered data collection and workflow processes, enabling an organization-wide flow of performance metrics and continual improvement programs.

Intelex's systems are 100 percent web-based and are available on an application service provider (ASP) model or as an in-house installation and are compatible with all industry-standard hardware and third-party software. Intelex systems delivery highly configurable user views, security, and organization-wide database maintenance all through the user interface. Intelex also leverages the latest in web-based technologies such as JavaScript and XML, which allows the system to operate on any standard web server without overwhelming system requirements.[1]

Q5 Systems Limited

Q5 promotes safety as their expertise. Q5AIMS was initially developed for the occupational safety and health user to help make the process of performing safety audits and inspections—and managing associated follow-up actions—faster, easier, and better.

Over time, Q5AIMS has evolved to incorporate many safety best-practice industry processes. The Q5 website notes that Q5 customers have performed thousands of safety audits, inspections, and assessments in almost every industry. Q5AIMS has been used for internal safety auditing, for federal and state OSHA compliance, industry-specific regulatory compliance, ad-hoc site inspections, behavior-based safety, and point-scoring systems. It has been used for aviation safety, marine safety, construction and manufacturing, warehousing, mining, oil field and well inspections, brewery facility inspections, forestry, loss control for insurance organizations, OHSAS 18001, and ILO guidelines-based checklists, to name a few.

Integrated Management System Auditing

Safety, quality, and environment are now often managed under the same banner for many companies. As a result, corporate auditing standards reflect a "best-practice" quality management approach because safety management systems have blended the elements and principles of quality management with what were previously prescriptive compliance standards. Q5's customers use Q5AIMS not only for safety assurance but also for management of quality and environmental audits and corrective action tracking. The corrective action process in Q5AIMS is patterned on the requirement for ISO 9001.

Q5 is perhaps the only integrated management system software company with its own internal management system developed and registered to the requirement of ISO 9001:2000.[2]

Steton Technology Group

Steton enterpriseINTELLIGENCE delivers a full range of enterprise information from detailed, multipage production reports to highly graphical business reports with the option of high-level dashboards (Steton Analytics). Business-intelligence reporting supplies accurate, relevant, and timely answers to business questions for more informed decision-making power.

Steton's website notes it is changing the way industry professionals manage quality, safety, regulatory compliance, and risk. Faster, more-accurate data collection is an immediate benefit of Steton, but the real advantages are early trend identification, automatically generated real-time reports, instant notification of noncompliant issues, and comprehensive corrective action management.[3]

CS Stars

CS STARS has been using technology to develop and support solutions for the risk and insurance marketplace. Their software and infrastructure are built with modern, industry-leading technologies to deliver security, scalability, and reliability. To give clients' maximum flexibility and value, CS STARS offers their suite of web-based products as either installed software or as hosted solutions that are fully supported and maintained by CS STARS.

CS STARS delivers comprehensive solutions for creating and performing business audits and compliance assessments. STARSTM AuditTM automates data collection, analysis, and recommendation tracking, helping clients gauge and maintain compliance with government regulations, environmental, health, and safety requirements, and other best practices. The following are some features of CS STARS software:

- Automated compliance assessments: Web-based tools streamline and standardize audits to ease data collection, reduce errors, and increase quality.

- Environmental, health, and safety audits: a library of templates to guide auditors through complex environmental, health, and safety audits. Templates are authored and maintained by a leading publisher of reference and interpretive material and offer detailed reference text to support auditors.

- Custom audits: Custom audits can be designed to gauge compliance with industry requirements, internal best practices, or any other criteria. These business audits use client-specific checklists, standards, workflow, and scoring methodologies.

- Create action plans and increase accountability: tools for documenting action items, assigning responsibility, and specifying target dates, budgets, and timelines. Action items can include file and image attachments to support remediation efforts or to evidence corrective action.

- Monitor remediation efforts and progress: A dashboard home page and reports enable managers to view outstanding action items, keep tabs on approaching target dates, and analyze trends in audit results. Reports can be automatically scheduled and distributed to internal and external stakeholders.[4]

Aon Safetylogic

Aon Safetylogic is a division of the Aon Corporation (AOC), a leading provider of risk management services, insurance and reinsurance brokerage, human capital and management consulting, and specialty insurance underwriting. Aon Safetylogic was founded in 1997 on the basis that occupational injuries and illnesses can be prevented. Safetylogic provides industry-leading and customizable web-based risk control compliance solutions. Their clients represent organizations of all sizes in a diverse set of industry sectors.

Their flagship solution, Safetylogic, is a feature-packed, risk-control-compliance solution for managing daily EH&S processes and data around auditing, self-inspections, recommendations tracking, injury/illness/OSHA/BLS reporting, safety meetings, surveys, bulletins, employee safety training, MSDS/chemical inventory management, and more. Clients subscribe to just the modules they desire, at the level that fits their organization.[5]

EtQ for Environmental Health and Safety (EHS)

EtQ's environmental health and safety (EHS) management system is a flexible software package that guides companies through compliance with ISO 14001, ISO 9000, OHSAS 18001, and similar standards for environmental health and safety management. Their web-browser-based system helps guide the user through the full lifecycle of achieving and maintaining EHS compliance. With EtQ's environmental health and safety software, all the information related to environmental health and safety compliance is easy to input, access, and report on. Document control, corrective action, audit management software, incidents, and EtQ's centralized reporting tool are just some of the dozens of processes EtQ's EHS software streamlines and simplifies.

EtQ is an integrated environmental health and safety management software system that has been preconfigured to specifically address the needs of EHS, ISO

9000, ISO 14001, and OHSAS 18001 processes. EtQ's unique modular approach provides unparalleled flexibility and automation. The modules are tightly integrated to deliver a best-in-class environmental management software solution. Connected to the production systems, EtQ connectors close the gap between production systems and the EHS software system. Modules like incidents and aspects connect to ERP and CRM systems to fully automate the creation and assignment of incidents without the need for additional incident-tracking software. Production systems can then be automatically updated throughout the incident resolution process. EtQ's unique EHS software system is designed to minimize the number of corrective actions using an advanced filtering model.

With all its functionality built around a common platform, EtQ has developed a unified environmental health and safety management system for handling processes in the environmental health and safety industry.[6]

The Harrington Group Quality Management Software

The Harrington Group is an advanced technology company that provides organizations of all sizes with quality management software solutions for their quality management and regulatory compliance needs. Enterprisewide global solutions as well as desktop products are available to support requirements such as corrective action/preventive action, document control, audits, customer complaints, supplier management, 21 CFR 11 compliance, root cause analysis, material nonconformance, training management, meeting management, opportunity for improvement, and much more. Harrington Group, Inc. (HGI) is a service-disabled-veteran-owned small business (SDVOSB) established in 1991 and headquartered in Orlando, Florida. Harrington Group is the pioneer and leading supplier of software tools for business/enterprise and quality management software solutions. The HGI team has a history of strong focus on quality and has developed a comprehensive set of management and technical processes based on ISO 9001:2000. The consistency achieved through the application of these processes provides the foundation for predictable performance and our reputation for delivering high-quality products, on time and within budget.[7]

IMPACT

Syntex Management Systems provide software and services that help companies protect worker health and safety, avoid devastating accidents, protect the environment, and cut costs. The world's leading companies use their flagship software product, Syntex IMPACT Enterprise, either in single-site locations or in worldwide deployments.

Syntex IMPACT Enterprise supports the customers' operational integrity initiatives. These initiatives are included in what is known today as enterprise risk management, operational risk management, and enterprise loss prevention. By deploying the software, customers save millions of dollars while at the same time improving worker productivity and product quality.

Furthermore, IMPACT Enterprise helps companies maintain critical regulatory compliance, such as environmental and OSHA regulations, while facilitating the companies' internal management systems, the International Organization for Standardization's management system standards, and the American Chemistry Council's Responsible Care® management system elements. It also facilitates the certification process of programs such as Occupational Safety and Health Administration's Voluntary Protection Programs, Star, Merit, and others.[8]

Amadeus—eQCM

The Amadeus software solution for enterprise quality and compliance management (eQCM®) is a web-based solution that enables organizations to comply with requirements stemming from ISO standards and manufacturing regulations (ISO 9001, ISO14001 GxP, FDA 21 CFR Part 11), financial reporting and governance regulations (SOx, CA Bill 198), and other industry standards and risk-based regulations. eQCM® is designed for maximum flexibility and easy adaptation to organizations' unique governance, compliance, and risk management (GRC) processes. eQCM® is helping organizations in a wide variety of sectors manage and control compliance and quality by automating processes such as document management, corrective and preventive actions, nonconformances and defects, complaints management, audits, training, incident management, corporate governance, and other related quality and business processes. eQCM® is also coupled with business intelligence capabilities, enterprise content management, and related technologies that help organizations achieve sustained compliance.[9]

Conclusion

The decision on whether or not to pursue a formal management system or a series of formal management systems into an integrated management system is one that should be made with careful thought, planning, and consideration of the value it will have for the business, its customers, employees, shareholders, and other stakeholders. Today, more than ever, increasing local, national, and international competition is rapidly changing the face of how business is being conducted in the "new economy." Any advantage in the way an organization does business is certainly important. Just as important is the way in which a business can structure its operations and management systems to support their sales, business objectives, and risk management initiatives and to leverage the knowledge and skills of their workforce to maximize their profits and minimize their loss.

A well-designed, well-run and effectively managed integrated management system is one of the linchpins in any successful business in the twenty-first century.

APPENDICES

The sources referenced in this appendix listing include practical tools and checklists that a reader can use, customize, or integrate into presentations to assist in the marketing and profile of the benefits of an integrated QHSE management system to their management team.

Appendix A

This is a sample QHSE Integrated Management System Audit Checklist that can be used or further customized to conduct a gap analysis against your existing management systems.

SAMPLE HSEQ INTEGRATED MANAGEMENT SYSTEM AUDIT CHECKLIST

Scope:		Audit Number:	
Auditee(s):		Audit Date:	
Audit Criteria:			
Lead Auditor: Additional Auditors:			
Attachments			
Regulations, Codes and/or Standards applicable to the audit and scope			
Additional management system elements for consideration in the audit: (i.e., Security, Process Safety Management, etc.)			

Scope and Application	OK	PP	OB	OFI	NC	NA

QMS (Quality Management System) Scope & Application
  a) Through the QMS, the company demonstrates its ability to consistently provide products that meet customer and applicable regulatory requirements?
  b) The company aims to enhance customer satisfaction through the effective application of the system, including processes for continual improvement of the system and the						

assurance of conformity to customer and applicable regulatory requirements? c) Are exclusions limited to requirements within clause 7 of QMS (Quality Management System)? d) Exclusions do not affect the organization's ability or responsibility to provide a product that meets: e) Customer requirements? f) Applicable regulatory requirements?						
SMS (Safety Management System) Scope & Application a) The OHS management system is applied to enable the company to control OHS risks and improve OHS performance? b) Scope and extent of the OHS management system is consistent with such factors as OHS policy, nature of activities, risks, and complexity of operations? c) OHS management system addresses occupational health and safety issues?						
EMS (Environmental Management System) Scope & Application d) The EMS environmental policy and objectives takes into account legal requirements and other requirements to which the company subscribes and information about significant environmental aspects? e) Environmental aspects can be controlled or influenced by the company? f) Scope and extent of the EMS is consistent with such factors as environmental policy, nature of activities, products, and services, and the location where and the conditions in which the company functions?						

OBJECTIVE EVIDENCE / COMMENTS

APPENDICES

References	O K	P P	O B	O F I	N C	N A
HSEQ Integrated Management System a) Are references and applicable codes, standards, and requirements identified?						

OBJECTIVE EVIDENCE / COMMENTS

Terms & Definitions	O K	P P	O B	O F I	N C	N A
HSEQ Integrated Management System a) Have the terms and definitions required for clear understanding of the management system documents been adequately defined?						

OBJECTIVE EVIDENCE / COMMENTS

General Requirements	O K	P P	O B	O F I	N C	N A

QMS (Quality Management System) General Requirements
a) Is the QMS established, documented, implemented, and maintained?
b) Is effectiveness of QMS continually improved in accordance with requirements of the QMS?
c) Does the company:
   • Identify the processes needed for the QMS and their application throughout the company?
   • Determine the sequence and interaction of these processes?
   • Determine the criteria and methods needed to ensure that both the operation and control of these processes are effective?
   • Ensure the availability of resources and information needed to support the operation and monitoring of these processes?
   • Monitor, measure, and analyze these processes?
   • Implement actions needed to achieve planned results and continual improvement of processes?
d) Are processes managed in accordance with the requirements of the QMS?
e) If processes that affect conformity with requirements are outsourced, does the company ensure control over these processes? How?
f) Is control of outsourced processes identified within the QMS?						

SMS (Safety Management System) General Requirements a) Has the company established, documented, implemented, maintained, and continually improved the OHS management system in accordance with the requirements of the safety management system and determined how it will fulfill the requirements? b) Has the scope of the OHS management system been defined and documented?						
EMS (Environmental Management System) General Requirements c) Has the company established, documented, implemented, maintained, and continually improved the EMS in accordance and determined how it will fulfill the requirements? d) Has the scope of the EMS been defined and documented?						

OBJECTIVE EVIDENCE / COMMENTS

Documentation Requirements	O K	P P	O B	O F I	N C	N A
QMS (Quality Management System) Documentation Requirements—General a) Does the QMS documentation include: • Quality policy? • Quality objectives? • Quality manual? • Documented procedures required by the quality management system? • Documents needed for effective planning, operation, and control of processes? • Records required by the quality management system? **QMS (Quality Management System) Quality Manual** a) Has a quality manual been established and maintained? b) Does it include: • Scope of the QMS? • Details and justification for any exclusions? • Documented procedures established for the QMS or references to them? • Description of the interaction between the processes of the QMS?						
SMS (Safety Management System) Documentation a) Does the OHS management system documentation include: • OHS policy? • OHS objectives and targets? • Description of the scope of the OHS management system? • Description of the main elements of the OHS management system and their interaction and reference to the related documents? • Documents, including records, required by the safety management system? • Documents, including records, determined to be necessary to ensure the effective planning, operation, and control of processes that relate to the management of its OHS risks? b) Is documentation proportional to the level of complexity, hazards, and risks concerned? c) Is documentation kept to the minimum required for effectiveness and efficiency?						
EMS (Environmental Management System) Documentation d) Does the EMS documentation include: • Environmental policy? • Environmental objectives and targets? • Description of the scope of the EMS? • Description of the main elements of the EMS and their interaction and reference to the related documents? • Documents, including records, required by the environmental management						

	OK	PP	OB	OFI	NC	NA
system?						
• Documents, including records, determined to be necessary to ensure the effective planning, operation, and control of processes that relate to the significant environmental aspects?						

OBJECTIVE EVIDENCE / COMMENTS

Control of Documents and Records	O K	P P	O B	O F I	N C	N A
QMS (Quality Management System) Control of Documents a) Are QMS documents effectively controlled? b) Is there a documented procedure developed and effectively implemented? Does it cover all requirements? c) Are QMS documents approved for adequacy prior to issue? d) Are controlled documents reviewed and updated, as necessary? Are revisions subject to reapproval? e) Are changes and current revision status of controlled documents identified? f) Are relevant versions of applicable documents available at points of use? g) Are controlled documents legible and readily identifiable? h) Are documents of external origin identified and their distribution controlled? i) Are obsolete documents identified and controlled to prevent their unintended use?						
SMS (Safety Management System) Control of Documents a) Are documents required by the OHS management system effectively controlled? b) Is there a documented procedure developed and effectively implemented? Does it cover all requirements? c) Are OHS management system documents approved for adequacy prior to issue? d) Are controlled documents reviewed and updated, as necessary? Are revisions subject to reapproval? e) Are changes and current revision status of controlled documents identified? f) Are relevant versions of applicable documents available at points of use? g) Are controlled documents legible and readily identifiable? h) Are documents of external origin that have been determined to be necessary for the planning and operation of the OHS management system identified and their distribution controlled? i) Are obsolete documents identified and controlled to prevent their unintended use?						
EMS (Environmental Management System) Control of Documents j) Are documents required by the EMS effectively controlled?						

k) Is there a documented procedure developed and effectively implemented? Does it cover all requirements? l) Are EMS documents approved for adequacy prior to issue? m) Are controlled documents reviewed and updated, as necessary? Are revisions subject to reapproval? n) Are changes and current revision status of controlled documents identified? o) Are relevant versions of applicable documents available at points of use? p) Are controlled documents legible and readily identifiable? q) Are documents of external origin that have been determined to be necessary for the planning and operation of the EMS identified and their distribution controlled? r) Are obsolete documents identified and controlled to prevent their unintended use?						

OBJECTIVE EVIDENCE / COMMENTS

Control of Documents and Records	O K	P P	O B	O F I	N C	N A
QMS (Quality Management System) Control of Records a) Are suitable records established and maintained to provide evidence of conformity to requirements and of the effective operation of the QMS? b) Are they legible, readily identifiable, and retrievable? c) Is there a documented procedure developed to define the controls needed for the identification, storage, protection, retrieval, retention time, and disposition of records? d) Is the procedure(s) effectively implemented?						
SMS (Safety Management System) Control of Records a) Are suitable records established and maintained to provide evidence of conformity to requirements of the OHS management system and the results achieved? b) Are they legible, readily identifiable, and traceable? c) Is there a documented procedure developed to define the controls needed for the identification, storage, protection, retrieval, retention time, and disposition of records? d) Is the procedure(s) effectively implemented?						
EMS (Environmental Management System) Control of Records a) Are suitable records established and maintained to provide evidence of conformity to requirements of the EMS and the results achieved? b) Are they legible, readily identifiable, and traceable? c) Is there a documented procedure developed to define the controls needed for the						

	identification, storage, protection, retrieval, retention time, and disposition of records?						
d)	Is the procedure(s) effectively implemented?						

OBJECTIVE EVIDENCE / COMMENTS

Management Leadership and Commitment, including Legal and Other Requirements	O K	P P	O B	O F I	N C	N A
QMS (Quality Management System) Management Commitment and Leadership a) Evidence for development and implementation of the QMS? b) Continual improvement of effectiveness? c) Communication of importance of meeting customer requirements, including statutory/regulatory requirements? d) Quality policy established? e) Quality objectives established? f) Management reviews conducted? g) Ensure availability of resources? **QMS (Quality Management System) Focus on the Customer** Have top management ensured that customer requirements are determined and are met with the aim of enhancing customer satisfaction? a) What measures are taken? Are they effective?						

OBJECTIVE EVIDENCE / COMMENTS

HSEQ Policies	O K	P P	O B	O F I	N C	N A
QMS (Quality Management System) Quality Policy a) Appropriate to the purpose of the organization? b) Includes a commitment to comply with requirements and continually improve the						

	effectiveness of the QMS?						
c)	Provides a framework for establishing and reviewing quality objectives?						
d)	Communicated and understood within the organization?						
e)	Reviewed for continuing suitability?						
	SMS (Safety Management System) Occupational Health & Safety Policy						
a)	Defined and authorized by senior management?						
b)	Established in consultation with workers and their representatives?						
c)	Appropriate to the nature, scale of OHS hazards and risks associated with organizational activities?						
d)	Includes a commitment to comply with applicable OHS legal requirements and other requirements to which company subscribes and which relate to workplace health and safety hazards?						
e)	Includes a commitment to prevent injury and work-related illnesses?						
f)	Includes a commitment to continually improve the OHS system and OHS performance?						
g)	Provides a framework for setting and reviewing OHS objectives?						
h)	Documented, implemented, and maintained?						
i)	Posted and communicated to all persons working in the organization to make them aware of their OHS obligations?						
j)	Available to interested parties, as appropriate?						
k)	Periodically reviewed to ensure that it remains relevant and appropriate?						
	EMS (Environmental Management System) Environmental Policy						
a)	Appropriate to the nature, scale, and environmental impacts of activities, products, services?						
b)	Includes a commitment to continual improvement and prevention of pollution?						
c)	Includes a commitment to comply with applicable legal requirements and other requirements to which the organization subscribes that relate to the environment?						
d)	Provides a framework for setting and reviewing environmental objectives and targets?						
e)	Documented, implemented, and maintained?						
f)	Communicated to all persons working for or on behalf of the organization?						
g)	Available to the public?						

OBJECTIVE EVIDENCE / COMMENTS

Objectives and Key Performance Indicators (KPI)	O K	P P	O B	O F I	N C	N A
QMS (Quality Management System) Objectives a) Established, by functions and levels? b) Measurable? c) Consistent with the quality policy? **QMS (Quality Management System) Planning** a) Quality management system planned to meet requirements and quality objectives? b) Integrity maintained when changes are planned and implemented?						

SMS (Safety Management System) OHS Objectives and Key Performance Indicators (KPI)
 	
a) Established, documented, implemented, and maintained by relevant functions and levels?
b) Measurable (where appropriated and practicable)?
c) Consistent with HSE policy, commitment to prevent injury or ill health, compliance with legal and other requirements, continual improvement?
d) Were/are legal and other requirements and OHS risks considered when establishing and reviewing objectives?
e) Are technological options, financial, operational, and business requirements and the views of interested parties considered when establishing and reviewing objectives?
f) Program established, implemented, and maintained to achieve objectives?
g) Does program include:
   • Designation of responsibility and authority for achieving objectives at relevant functions and levels of the company?
   • Means and time frame by which objectives are to be achieved?
h) Is the program reviewed at regular and planned intervals?
i) Are intervals adjusted, as necessary, to ensure that objectives are achieved?						

EMS (Environmental Management System) Environmental Objectives and Key Performance Indicators (KPI) a) Established by functions and levels? b) Measurable? c) Consistent with environmental policy (including commitment to prevent pollution, comply with legal and other requirements)? d) Take into account legal requirements, significant aspects, technological options, financial, operational, and business requirements, and the views of interested parties? e) Program in place to achieve objectives? f) Roles and responsibilities for achievement of objectives established? g) Means and time frame for achievement established?						

OBJECTIVE EVIDENCE / COMMENTS

Environmental Aspects & Impacts	O K	P P	O B	O F I	N C	N A
EMS (Environmental Management System) Environmental Aspects and Impacts a) Documented procedure? b) Environmental aspects identified for all activities, products, services within scope of EMS and those that it can influence? c) Aspects take into account planned or new developments, new or modified activities, products, or services? d) Has organization determined those aspects that have or can have SIGNIFICANT environmental impact? e) Aspects and impacts documented and up to date? f) Aspects and impacts taken into account when establishing, implementing, and maintaining the EMS?						

OBJECTIVE EVIDENCE / COMMENTS

Hazard and Risk Assessment and Control	O K	P P	O B	O F I	N C	N A

SMS (Safety Management System) Hazard and Risk Assessment and Controls
 	
a) Procedure in place for the ongoing hazard identification, risk assessment, and determination of necessary records?
b) Does hazard and risk identification procedure take into account:
  • Routine and nonroutine activities?
  • Activities of all persons having access to the workplace (including contractors and visitors)?
  • Human behavior, capabilities, and other human factors?
  • Identified hazards originating outside the workplace capable of adversely affecting the health and safety of persons under the control of the organization in the workplace?
  • Hazards created in the vicinity of the workplace by work-related activities under the control of the company (including environmental aspects)?
  • Infrastructure, equipment, and materials at the workplace, whether provided by the organization or others?						

• Changes or proposed changes in the organization, its activities, or materials?							

- • Changes or proposed changes in the organization, its activities, or materials?
- • Modifications to the OHS management system, including temporary changes and their impacts on operations, processes, and activities?
- • Any applicable legal obligations relating to risk assessment and implementation of necessary controls?
- • The design of work areas, processes, installations, machinery/equipment, operating procedures, and work organization, including their adaptation to human capabilities?

c) Is the methodology for hazard identification and risk assessment defined with respect to the scope, nature, and timing to be proactive vs. reactive?

d) Does the methodology provide for the identification, prioritization, and documentation of risks and the application of controls, as appropriate?

e) Management of change: Are the OHS hazards and OHS risks associated with changes in the company, the OHS system, or its activities identified prior to introducing the changes?

f) How are the results of these assessments considered when deciding upon appropriate controls?

g) When developing or changing controls to manage risk, is the following hierarchy applied:
- • Elimination
- • Substitution
- • Engineering controls
- • Signage/Warnings/Administrative controls
- • Personal protective equipment

h) Are the results of hazard identification, risk assessment, and established controls documented and maintained up to date?

i) Are the OHS risks and controls taken into account when establishing, implementing, and maintaining the OHS management system?

OBJECTIVE EVIDENCE / COMMENTS

Responsibility, Authority & Communication	O K	P P	O B	O F I	N C	N A
QMS (Quality Management System) Responsibility and Authority a) Are responsibilities and authorities defined, documented, and communicated?						

SMS (Safety Management System) Responsibility and Authority
 	
   a) Does top management take ultimate responsibility for the OHS and OHS management system?
   b) Does top management demonstrate commitment by defining roles, allocating responsibilities and accountabilities, and delegating authorities to facilitate effective OHS management?
   c) Are roles, responsibilities, accountabilities, and authorities documented and communicated?
   d) Do all those with management responsibility demonstrate their commitment to continual improvement of the OHS?
   e) How does the company ensure that all persons take responsibility for aspects of the OHS they control, including adherence to the OHS requirements?						

EMS (Environmental Management System) Responsibility and Authority a) Are responsibilities and authorities defined, documented, and communicated?						

OBJECTIVE EVIDENCE / COMMENTS

Management Representative	O K	P P	O B	O F I	N C	N A

QMS (Quality Management System) Management Representative
 	
   a) Management representative appointed by top management?
   b) Has responsibility and authority to ensure that processes needed for QMS are						

	OK	PP	OB	OFI	NC	NA
established, implemented, and maintained? c) Reports to top management on performance of QMS and need for improvement? d) Ensures the promotion of awareness of customer requirements throughout the company? e) Liaises with external parties on matters relating to QMS?						

SMS (Safety Management System) Management Representative
a) Has a management representative been appointed from top management who has specific responsibility for OHS?
b) Does management representative have defined role and responsibility to:
   • Ensure that the OHS management system is established, implemented, and maintained in accordance with ISO 18001?
   • Report to top management on performance of OHS system?
   • Ensure that reports to management are used as a basis for improvement to the OHS system?
c) Is identity of the management representative available to all persons working under the control of the company?						

EMS (Environmental Management System) Management Representative a) Management representative appointed? b) Has responsibility and authority to ensure that EMS is established, implemented, and maintained? c) Reports to management on EMS performance and need for improvement?						

OBJECTIVE EVIDENCE / COMMENTS

Communication	OK	PP	OB	OFI	NC	NA
QMS (Quality Management System) Communication a) Appropriate communication processes established? b) Does communication take place regarding the effectiveness of the QMS?						
SMS (Safety Management System) Communication						

APPENDICES

Communication							

a) Procedure established and implemented in relation to OHS hazards and the OHS system for:
   • Internal communication among the various levels and functions of the organization?
   • Communication with contractors and other visitors to the workplace?
   • Receiving, documenting, and responding to relevant communications from external interested parties?
 	
Participation and Consultation
a) Procedure established and implemented for participation of workers by:
   • Involvement, as appropriate, in hazard identification, risk assessments, and determination of controls?
   • Involvement in incident investigations, as appropriate?
   • Involvement in development and review of OHS policies and objectives?
   • Consultation where there are any changes that affect their OHS?
   • Representation on OHS matters?
 	
b) Are workers informed about their participation arrangements, including who is their representative(s) on OHS matters? Included in procedure?
c) How are contractors consulted where there are changes that affect their OHS? Included in procedure?
d) What are the provisions for consulting relevant external interested parties, when appropriate, regarding pertinent OHS matters?							

EMS (Environmental Management System) Communication
a) **Procedure** and process for:
   • Internal communication among various levels and functions in the company regarding environmental aspects and the EMS?
   • Receiving, documenting, and responding to relevant communication from external interested parties?
 	
b) Have any decisions regarding whether to communicate externally regarding significant environmental aspects been documented? If so, what was the method developed for this external communication?							

OBJECTIVE EVIDENCE / COMMENTS

Management Review	O K	P P	O B	O F I	N C	N A
QMS (Quality Management System) Management Review						
a) Does management review of the QMS take place at planned intervals?						
b) Does it address:						
• Suitability?						
• Adequacy?						
• Effectiveness?						
• Opportunities for improvement?						
• Need for changes to QMS?						
• Need for changes to quality policy and objectives?						
c) Are records of management review maintained?						
Review Input						
a) Does input to management review include:						
• Results of internal and external audits?						
• Customer feedback?						
• Information on process and product conformity, including status of NCRs?						
• Status of corrective and preventive actions?						
• Follow-up on action items from previous management review?						
• Changes that could affect the QMS?						
• Recommendations for improvement?						
Review Output						
a) Does output from management review include decisions and actions related to:						
• Improvement of the effectiveness of the QMS and its processes?						
• Improvement of product related to customer requirements?						
• Resource needs?						

OBJECTIVE EVIDENCE / COMMENTS

Management Review	O K	P P	O B	O F I	N C	N A

SMS (Safety Management System) Management Review
a) Does management review of the OHS system take place at planned intervals?
b) Does it address:
    • Suitability?
    • Adequacy?
    • Effectiveness?
    • Opportunities for improvement?
    • Need for changes to OHS system?
    • Need for changes to HSE policy and objectives?
 	
c) Are records of management review of EMS maintained?
d) Does input to OHS system management review include:
    • Results of internal and external audits and evaluations of compliance with legal and other requirements to which company subscribes?
    • Results of participation and consultation?
    • Relevant communication from external interested parties, including complaints?
    • OHS performance of the company?
    • Extent to which objectives have been met?
    • Status of incident investigations, corrective, and preventive actions?
    • Follow-up on action items from previous management review?
    • Changing circumstances, including developments in legal and other requirements related to OHS?
    • Recommendations for improvement?
 	
e) Is output from management review of OHS systems consistent with commitment to continual improvement?
 	
f) Does output include decisions and actions related to possible changes to OHS performance, OHS policies and objectives, resources, other elements of the OHS management system?
 	
g) Are relevant outputs from management review of the OHS system made available for communication and consultation?						

OBJECTIVE EVIDENCE / COMMENTS

Management Review	O K	P P	O B	O F I	N C	N A

EMS (Environmental Management System) Management Review
a) Does management review of the EMS take place at planned intervals?
b) Does it address:
   • Suitability?
   • Adequacy?
   • Effectiveness?
   • Opportunities for improvement?
   • Need for changes to EMS?
   • Need for changes to environmental policy, objectives, and *targets*?
 	
c) Are records of management review of EMS maintained?
d) Does input to EMS management review include:
   • Results of internal and external audits and evaluations of compliance with legal and other requirements to which company subscribes?
   • Communication from external interested parties, including complaints?
   • Environmental performance of the company?
   • Extent to which objectives and targets have been met?
   • Status of corrective and preventive actions?
   • Follow-up on action items from previous management review?
   • Changing circumstances, including developments in legal and other requirements related to environmental aspects?
   • Recommendations for improvement?
 	
e) Does output from management review of EMS include decisions and actions related to possible changes to the environmental policy, objectives, targets, and other elements of the EMS consistent with the commitment to continual improvement?						

OBJECTIVE EVIDENCE / COMMENTS

Resources	O K	P P	O B	O F I	N C	N A
QMS (Quality Management System) Resources **General** a) Resources determined and provided? b) To implement and maintain the QMS and to continually improve its effectiveness? c) To enhance customer satisfaction by meeting customer requirements? **Infrastructure** a) Is infrastructure required to achieve product/service conformity determined, provided, and maintained? This includes buildings, work space, associated utilities, process equipment (hardware and software), supporting services (transport, communication). **Working Environment (See section of the Safety Management System)** a) Is the work environment required to achieve product/service conformity determined and managed?						
SMS (Safety Management System) Roles and Responsibility a) Does top management demonstrate commitment by ensuring availability of resources essential to establish, implement, maintain, and improve the OHS system? (Including human resources, specialized skills, organizational infrastructure, technology and financial resources.)						
EMS (Environmental Management System) Roles and Responsibility a) Has management ensured availability of resources essential to establish, implement, maintain, and improve the EMS? (Including human resources, specialized skills, organizational infrastructure, technology, and financial resources.)						

OBJECTIVE EVIDENCE / COMMENTS

Human Resource Management	O K	P P	O B	O F I	N C	N A
QMS (Quality Management System) Human Resource Management						
a) Have competency requirements been determined?						
b) Where necessary, is training provided or other action taken to satisfy competency requirements?						
c) Is the effectiveness of training or action to develop competency evaluated?						
d) Are appropriate records of education, training, skills, and experience kept?						
e) Are personnel aware of the relevance and importance of their activities and how they contribute to the achievement of quality objectives?						
SMS (Safety Management Training) Training						
a) How does the company ensure that persons performing tasks that can impact on OHS are competent on the basis of appropriate education, training, or experience?						
b) How does the company identify training needs associated with the OHS risks and OHS management system?						
c) Is required training or other action taken to meet these needs?						
d) How is the effectiveness of training or action evaluated?						
e) Are appropriate records of OHS-related education, training, skills, and experience kept?						
f) Do we have procedure(s), and do we make people under our control aware of:						
• The OHS consequences, actual or potential, of their work activities, their behavior, and the OHS benefits of improved personal performance?						
• Roles & responsibilities and importance in achieving conformity to the OHS policy, procedures, and requirements of the OHS system, including emergency preparedness and response requirements?						
• Potential consequences of departure from specified procedures?						
g) Do training procedures take into account differing levels of responsibility, ability, language skills and literacy, and *risk*?						
EMS (Environmental Management System) Training						
a) Are persons performing tasks that have the potential to cause a significant environmental impact(s) competent on the basis of appropriate education, training, or experience?						
b) How do we identify training needs associated with environmental aspects and EMS?						
c) Are appropriate records of EMS-related education, training, skills, and experience kept?						
d) Do we have a documented procedure, and do we make people working for us or on our behalf aware of:						
• The importance of conformity to the environmental policy and procedures and the EMS?						
• Significant aspects and impacts associated with their work and benefits of improved						

personal performance?						
• Roles & responsibilities in achieving conformity with the requirements of the EMS?						
• Potential consequences of departure from specified procedures?						

OBJECTIVE EVIDENCE / COMMENTS

Products and Services	O K	P P	O B	O F I	N C	N A
QMS (Quality Management System) Product Planning a) Processes for product realization planned and developed, consistent with requirements of other QMS processes? b) Does planning determine: • Quality objectives and requirements for the product? • Need for processes, documents, and resources required for the product? • Required verification, validation, monitoring, inspection, and tests specific to product; acceptance criteria? • Records to provide evidence of fulfilled requirements? c) Is the output from planning suitable for the organization's method of operations?						

OBJECTIVE EVIDENCE / COMMENTS

Requirement of the Customer	O K	P P	O B	O F I	N C	N A
QMS (Quality Management System) Customer Requirements **7.2.1 Determination of Requirements Related to the Product** a) Does the company determine: • Requirements specified by the customer (including those for delivery and post-delivery activities)? • Unstated but necessary for specified or intended use?						

172

• Statutory and regulatory requirements? • Additional requirements determined by the company?						

7.2.2 Review of Requirements Related to the Product
a) Are product requirements reviewed prior to commitment (i.e., submission of tender, acceptance of contract or order, acceptance of changes to contract or order)?
b) Does contract review ensure that:
   • Product requirements are defined?
   • Differences are resolved?
   • Company has the ability to meet defined requirements?
c) Are records of the results of review and actions arising from the review maintained?
d) Where there is no documented statement of requirement, how are customer requirements confirmed before acceptance?
e) When requirements are changed, are documents amended and people informed of the required changes?						

SMS (Safety Management Systems) Legal Requirements a) Procedure in place to identify and ensure access to legal requirements and other applicable OHS requirements? b) Procedure implemented and effective? c) Have applicable legal requirements and other requirements been incorporated into the OHS system? How? d) Is information up to date? e) Relevant information on legal and other requirements communicated to persons working under control of the organization and other relevant parties?						
EMS (Environmental Management System) Legal Requirements a) Procedure in place to identify and access applicable legal requirements and other requirement to which the organization subscribes related to environmental aspects and how these requirements apply to the organizational environmental aspects? Procedure implemented and effective? b) Legal and other requirements taken into account when establishing, implementing, and maintaining the EMS? How?						

OBJECTIVE EVIDENCE / COMMENTS

Communication with the Customer	O K	P P	O B	O F I	N C	N A
QMS (Quality Management System) Customer Communication a) Are arrangements determined and implemented for communicating with customers in relation to: • Product information? • Inquiries, contracts, or order handling, including amendments? • Customer feedback, including complaints?						
SMS (Safety Management System) Communication, Participation, and Consultation (see section 5)						
EMS (Environmental Management System) Communication (see section 5)						

OBJECTIVE EVIDENCE / COMMENTS

Design and Development	O K	P P	O B	O F I	N C	N A
QMS (Quality Management System) Section 7.3.1 Design and Development Planning a) Is design and development planned and controlled? b) During design planning, does the company determine: • The design and development stages? • The review, verification, and validation activities appropriate to each design stage? • Responsibilities and authorities for the design? c) Are interfaces managed for effective communication and assignment of responsibility? d) Is design output updated as the design progresses?						
QMS (Quality Management System) Section 7.3.2 Design and Development Inputs a) Are inputs relating to product requirements determined and recorded? b) Do inputs include:						

	O K	P P	O B	O F I	N C	N A
• Functional and performance requirements? • Statutory and regulatory requirements? • Information from previous similar designs, if applicable? • Other requirements essential to the design? c) Are inputs reviewed for adequacy? d) Are requirements completely unambiguous and not conflicting?						
QMS (Quality Management System) Section 7.3.3 Design and Development Outputs a) Are outputs in a form which is verifiable against input and approved prior to issue and release? b) Do outputs: • Meet input requirements? • Provide appropriate information for purchasing, production, and service provision? • Contain or reference product acceptance criteria? • Specify characteristics essential for safe and proper use?						

OBJECTIVE EVIDENCE / COMMENTS

Design and Development	O K	P P	O B	O F I	N C	N A
QMS (Quality Management System) Section 7.3.4 Design and Development Review a) Are systematic reviews of design and development performed at suitable stages, in accordance with planned arrangements (see 7.3.1)? b) Do the reviews: • Evaluate the ability of results of design and development to meet requirements? • Identify any problems and propose necessary changes? c) Do design reviews include representatives of functions concerned with the design stage being reviewed? d) Are records of design review and any necessary actions maintained?						
QMS (Quality Management System) Section 7.3.5 Design and Development Verification a) Is verification of design outputs against input requirements performed in accordance with planned arrangements? b) Are results of verification and required actions recorded?						

QMS (Quality Management System) Section 7.3.6 Design and Development Validation
  a) Is design validation performed in accordance with planned arrangements to ensure that resulting product is capable of meeting the requirements for specified application or intended use, where known?
  b) Is validation completed prior to delivery or implementation of the product, where practicable?
  c) Are results of validation and required actions recorded?						

QMS (Quality Management System) Section 7.3.7 Control of Design and Development Changes
  a) Are design changes identified and recorded?
  b) Are changes reviewed, verified, and validated, as appropriate, and approved prior to implementation?
  c) Does review include evaluation of the effect of changes on constituent parts and product already delivered?
  d) Are results of the review of changes and necessary actions recorded?						

OBJECTIVE EVIDENCE / COMMENTS

Purchasing & Management of Supplier and Vendors	O K	P P	O B	O F I	N C	N A

QMS (Quality Management System) Supplier and Vendor Approval and Review Process
  a) How does the company ensure that purchased products / services conform to specified purchase requirements?
  b) Is there evidence that the extent and type of control is dependent upon effect of the purchased product on subsequent product realization/final product?
  c) Are suppliers evaluated and selected based on their ability to supply product that meets requirements?
  d) Is the criteria for selection, evaluation, and re-evaluation of suppliers established?
  e) Are records maintained of evaluations and any necessary actions arising from them?						

QMS (Quality Management System) Purchasing
  a) Does purchasing information describe product?
  b) Does the information include (as appropriate):
    • Requirements for approval of products, procedures, processes, equipment?
    • Requirements for qualification of personnel?
    • Quality management system requirements?
  c) Is the adequacy of the specified purchase requirements verified prior to communication with the supplier?						

	O K	P P	O B	O F I	N C	N A
QMS (Quality Management System) Purchased Product Verification a) Are inspection activities established and implemented to verify purchased product against specified requirements? b) Where the company or the customer intends to perform verification at the supplier's premises, are the intended verification arrangements and method of product release specified in the purchasing information?						
SMS (Safety Management System) Controls a) Has the company implemented and maintained controls related to purchased goods, equipment, and services? (see section 7, Planning of Product Realization)						
EMS (Environmental Management System) Controls a) How do we communicate our procedures and requirements associated with our environmental aspects and impacts to our contractors and suppliers? (see section 7, Planning of Product Realization)						

OBJECTIVE EVIDENCE / COMMENTS

Products and Services	O K	P P	O B	O F I	N C	N A
QMS (Quality Management System) Production and Service a) Is production and service provision planned and carried out under controlled conditions? b) Are controls effectively implemented, including: • Information that describes the characteristics of the product? • Availability of work instructions, as required? • Use of suitable equipment? • Availability and use of monitoring and measuring devices? • Implementation of monitoring and measurement? • Implementation of release, delivery, and postdelivery activities?						

SMS (Safety Management System) Control of Risk
a) Has company determined the operations and activities associated with identified hazards (where the implementation of control is necessary to manage OHS risks)?
b) Are there processes established to manage change?
c) Has the company implemented and maintained:
    • Operational controls, as applicable to the company and its activities. Are the operational controls integrated into overall OHS management system?
    • Controls related to purchased goods, equipment, and services?
    • Controls related to contractors and other visitors to the workplace?
    • Documented procedures to cover situations where their absence could lead to deviations from the HSE policy and objectives?
    • Stipulated operating criteria where their absence could lead to deviations from the HSE policy?							

EMS (Environmental Management System) Control of Environmental Risk a) Operations associated with identified significant environmental aspects identified and planned to ensure that they are carried out under specified conditions? b) Is planning consistent with environmental policy, objectives, and targets? c) Documented procedures established, implemented, and maintained to control situations where their absence could lead to deviation from the environmental policy and targets? d) Procedures stipulate operating criteria? e) Procedures related to the identified significant environmental aspects of goods and services used by the company established, implemented, and maintained? f) Procedures and applicable requirements communicated to suppliers and contractors?							

OBJECTIVE EVIDENCE / COMMENTS

Products and Services	O K	P P	O B	O F I	N C	N A
QMS (Quality Management System) Product Verification a) Are there any processes where the resulting output cannot be verified by subsequent monitoring or measurement? (Including processes where deficiencies only become apparent after the product is in use or the service has been delivered.) b) Are these processes validated to demonstrate that the processes are capable of achieving planned results? c) Have arrangements for these processes been made, including:						

• Defined criteria for review and approval of the processes? • Approval of equipment? • Qualification of personnel? • Use of specific methods and procedures? • Requirements for records? • Revalidation?						
QMS (Quality Management System) Product Tracking a) Has product been identified by suitable means, where appropriate, throughout product realization? b) Is product status identified with respect to monitoring and measurement requirements? c) Is traceability a requirement? d) If so, is the unique identification of the product controlled and recorded? (e.g., configuration management)						
QMS (Quality Management System) Control of Customer-Owned Property a) Is customer property under the company's control or used in the provision of the final product or service to the customer? b) If so, how is this property identified? c) How is it verified? d) How is it protected and safeguarded? e) What provision is made for recording and reporting to the customer when customer property is lost, damaged, or otherwise found to be unsuitable for use? f) How is customer intellectual property safeguarded and protected?						

QMS (Quality Management System) Integrity of Customer-Owned Property
a) Is product conformity preserved during internal processing and delivery to the intended destination?
b) Does preservation include:
   • Identification?
   • Handling?
   • Packaging?
   • Storage?
   • Protection?
c) Have adequate arrangements for preservation been applied to the constituent parts of the product?						

OBJECTIVE EVIDENCE / COMMENTS

Monitoring and Measuring Devices	O K	P P	O B	O F I	N C	N A
QMS (Quality Management System) Monitoring and Measuring Devices a) Has required monitoring and measurement, and measuring devices needed, been determined? b) Are processes in place to ensure that monitoring and measurement is carried out in a manner that is consistent with the requirements established? c) Where necessary to ensure valid results, the measuring equipment is: • Calibrated at specified intervals or prior to use against traceable national or international standards or recorded alternate verification methods? • Adjusted or readjusted as necessary? • Identified to determine calibration status? • Safeguarded from adjustments that would invalidate results? • Protected from damage and deterioration during handling, maintenance, and storage? d) Are previous measuring results assessed for validity when equipment is found nonconforming? Are appropriate actions taken on affected equipment and product? e) Are calibration and verification records maintained? f) When used in monitoring and measurement of specified requirements, is computer software ability for intended application confirmed prior to initial use and reconfirmed as necessary?						
SMS (Safety Management System) Safety Performance Measurement a) Is equipment required to monitor and measure OHS performance? b) If so, are appropriate procedures in place for calibration and maintenance of equipment? c) Are records of calibration and maintenance activities and results maintained?						
EMS (Environmental Management System) Environmental Performance Measurement a) Is equipment required to monitor and measure environmental performance/compliance? b) If so, is calibrated and verified monitoring and measuring equipment used and maintained? c) Are records of calibration and maintenance activities and results maintained?						

OBJECTIVE EVIDENCE / COMMENTS

Measurement and Compliance Evaluation	O K	P P	O B	O F I	N C	N A
QMS (Quality Management System) a) Monitoring, measurement, analysis, and improvement processes planned and implemented as needed to: • Demonstrate product conformity? • Ensure quality management system conformity? • Continually improve the effectiveness of the quality management system? b) Applicable methods (including statistical techniques) and extent of their use determined?						
QMS (Quality Management System) Monitoring and Measurement a) Suitable methods for monitoring and measurement of the quality management system processes applied? b) Methods demonstrate ability of the processes to achieve planned results? c) Corrective action taken to ensure conformity of the product when planned results not achieved?						
QMS (Quality Management System) Monitoring and Measurement a) Characteristics of the product to verify product requirements are met, monitored, and measured? b) Carried out at appropriate stages of product realization process? c) Evidence of conformity with acceptance criteria maintained? d) Records indicate person authorizing release of product? e) Product release and service delivery do not proceed until all planned arrangements have been satisfactorily completed unless otherwise approved by relevant authority and customer (if applicable)?						

OBJECTIVE EVIDENCE / COMMENTS

Monitoring and Measuring / Evaluation of Compliance	O K	P P	O B	O F I	N C	N A
SMS (Safety Management System) Safety Performance Measurement a) Is there a procedure, and do we monitor and measure, on a regular basis, OHS performance? b) Does procedure and practice address: • Both qualitative and quantitative measures appropriate to the needs of the company? • Monitoring of the extent to which the OHS objectives are met? • Monitoring the effectiveness of controls for health and safety? • Proactive measures of performance that monitor conformance with OHS program, controls, and operational criteria? • Reactive measures of performance that monitor ill health, incidents (including accidents, near misses, etc.), and other historical evidence of deficient OHS performance? • Recording of data and results of monitoring and measurement sufficient to facilitate subsequent corrective action and preventive action analysis? **SMS (Safety Management System) Compliance Evaluation** a) Is there a procedure for periodically evaluating compliance with applicable legal requirements? b) Do we evaluate compliance with other requirements to which the company subscribes? c) Records of results of periodic evaluations?						
EMS (Environmental Management System) Monitoring and Measurement a) Is there a procedure, and do we monitor and measure, on a regular basis, the key characteristics of operations that can have significant environmental impact? b) Does a procedure and practice address performance monitoring, applicable operational controls, and conformity with environmental objectives and targets? **EMS (Environmental Management System) Compliance Evaluation** a) Is there a **procedure** for periodically evaluating compliance with applicable legal requirements? b) Do we evaluate compliance with other requirements to which the company subscribes? c) Records of results of periodic evaluations?						

OBJECTIVE EVIDENCE / COMMENTS

Customer Satisfaction	O K	P P	O B	O F I	N C	N A

QMS (Quality Management System) Customer Satisfaction
  a) Customer perception information and customer fulfilment of requirements monitored?
  b) Methods to obtain information determined?						

OBJECTIVE EVIDENCE / COMMENTS

Audit of the Management Systems	O K	P P	O B	O F I	N C	N A

QMS (Quality Management System) Internal Audit
  a) Internal audits conducted at planned intervals to determine that the QMS:
    • Conforms to planned arrangements?
    • Conforms to QMS and the company's established requirements?
    • Is effectively implemented and maintained?
 	
  b) Audit program planned, implemented, and maintained considering the status and importance of processes, areas, and results of previous audits?
  c) Audit criteria, scope, frequency, and methods defined?
  d) Auditor's objectivity and impartiality ensured?
  e) Auditors do not audit their own work?
  f) Documented procedure (Responsibilities and requirements for planning and conducting audits? Reporting results? Maintaining records?)?
  g) Management responsible for the audited area ensures that actions are taken without undue delay to eliminate nonconformities and their causes?
  h) Follow-up activities include verification of the actions taken and the reporting of results?						

OBJECTIVE EVIDENCE / COMMENTS

Internal Audit	O K	P P	O B	O F I	N C	N A

SMS (Safety Management System) Internal Audit
a) Internal audits conducted at planned intervals to determine whether the OHS management system:
   • Conforms to planned arrangements for OHS management, including the safety management system?
   • Is effectively implemented and maintained?
   • Is effective in meeting the HSE policy and OHS objectives?
 	
b) Audit results provided to management?
c) Audit program planned, carried out, and maintained based upon risk assessments of the company's activities and the results of previous audits?
d) Documented procedure addresses:
   • Responsibilities, competencies, and requirements for planning and conducting audits, reporting results, and retaining associated records?
   • Determining audit criteria, scope, frequency, and methods?
e) Auditors' objectivity and impartiality ensured?						

EMS (Environmental Management System) Internal Audit
a) Internal audits conducted at planned intervals to determine that the EMS:
   • Conforms to planned arrangements for environmental management?
   • Is effectively implemented and maintained?
 	
b) Audit results provided to management?
c) Audit program planned, carried out, and maintained considering the environmental importance of operations concerned and results of previous audits?
d) Documented procedure addresses:
   • Responsibilities and requirements for planning and conducting audits, reporting results, and retaining associated records?
   • Determining audit criteria, scope, frequency, and methods?
e) Auditors' objectivity and impartiality ensured?						

OBJECTIVE EVIDENCE / COMMENTS

Management of Nonconformance	O K	P P	O B	O F I	N C	N A

QMS (Quality Management System) Product Nonconformance
a) Documented procedure defines the controls and related responsibilities and authorities for dealing with nonconforming product?
b) Is product (outcome of ANY process) not conforming to requirements identified and controlled to prevent its unintended use or delivery?
c) Appropriate action taken to deal with nonconformity, i.e.:
   • Action to eliminate the nonconformity?
   • Authorized use of nonconforming product?
   • Release or acceptance under concession by relevant authority?
   • Action to preclude original intended use or application?
d) Are records maintained regarding the nature of nonconformities and subsequent actions taken, including concessions obtained?
e) Is nonconforming product that has been corrected subject to reverification to demonstrate conformity to requirements?
f) Is action appropriate to the effects or potential effects when nonconforming product is detected after delivery or use?
g) Does the nonconformance control process include process, service, procedural nonconformances?						

OBJECTIVE EVIDENCE / COMMENTS

Management of Nonconformance	O K	P P	O B	O F I	N C	N A
SMS (Safety Management System) Action Tracking a) Procedure for dealing with actual and potential nonconformity and for taking corrective action and preventive action? b) Nonconformances identified and corrected? c) Action taken to mitigate OHS consequences? d) Nonconformances investigated to determine causes and action taken to avoid recurrence? e) Need for action evaluated to prevent nonconformances and action taken to avoid occurrence? f) Results of corrective and preventive action recorded and communicated? g) Effectiveness of corrective and preventive action reviewed?						

	OK	PP	OB	OFI	NC	NA
h) Where CA/PA identifies new or changed hazards or the need for new or changed controls, the procedure required that proposed actions are taken through a risk assessment prior to implementation? i) Are necessary changes arising from CA/PA made to the OHS documentation?						
EMS (Environmental Management System) Action Tracking a) Procedure for dealing with actual and potential nonconformity and for taking corrective action and preventive action? b) Nonconformances identified and corrected? c) Action taken to mitigate environmental impacts? d) Nonconformances investigated to determine causes and action taken to avoid recurrence? e) Need for action evaluated to prevent nonconformances and action taken to avoid occurrence? f) Results of corrective and preventive action recorded? g) Effectiveness of corrective and preventive action reviewed? h) Are actions taken appropriate to the magnitude of the problems and the environmental impacts encountered? i) Are necessary changes made to the EMS documentation?						

OBJECTIVE EVIDENCE / COMMENTS

Analysis of Data	O K	P P	O B	O F I	N C	N A
QMS (Quality Management System) Analysis of Data a) Is data that demonstrates suitability and effectiveness of the QMS: • Determined? • Collected? • Analyzed? b) Is data used to evaluate where continual improvement of the effectiveness of the QMS can be made? c) Does this include data generated as a result of monitoring and measurement and from other relevant sources?						

	OK	PP	OB	OFI	NC	NA
d) Does data analysis provide information relating to: • Customer satisfaction? • Conformity to requirements? • Characteristics and trends of processes and products, including opportunities for preventive action? • Suppliers and vendors?						

OBJECTIVE EVIDENCE / COMMENTS

Continual Improvement and Action Tracking	OK	PP	OB	OFI	NC	NA

QMS (Quality Management System) Continual Improvement
a) Does the company continually improve the effectiveness of the QMS through the use of the:
  a) Quality policy?
  b) Quality objectives?
  c) Audit results?
  d) Analysis of data?
  e) Corrective and preventive actions?
  f) Management review?						

QMS (Quality Management System) Corrective Action
 	
a) Is action taken to eliminate the cause of nonconformances in order to prevent recurrence?
b) Corrective action appropriate to the effects of the nonconformances encountered?
c) Procedure established and implemented that defines requirements for:
  • Reviewing causes of nonconformances (including customer complaints)?
  • Determining the causes of the nonconformances?
  • Evaluating the need for action to ensure that nonconformances do not recur?
  • Determining and implementing action needed?
  • Recording results of action taken?
  • Reviewing corrective action taken?						

QMS (Quality Management System)- Preventive Action a) Is action taken to eliminate the cause of potential nonconformances in order to prevent						

187

occurrence?							
b) Preventive action appropriate to the effects of the potential problems?							
c) Procedure established *and implemented* that defines requirements for:							
• Identifying potential nonconformances and their causes?							
• Evaluating the need for action to ensure that nonconformances do not occur?							
• Determining and implementing action needed?							
• Recording results of action taken?							
• Reviewing preventive action taken?							

OBJECTIVE EVIDENCE / COMMENTS

Emergency Preparedness and Response	O K	P P	O B	O F I	N C	N A
SMS (Safety Management System) Emergency Preparedness and Response						
a) Has a procedure been established to identify the potential for and responses to incidents and emergency situations?						
b) Is procedure implemented and maintained effectively?						
c) Company responds to actual emergency situations and prevents or mitigates associated adverse OHS consequences? How?						
d) In planning emergency exercises, are the needs of relevant interested parties (e.g., emergency services and neighbors) taken into account?						
e) Are periodic emergency response tests carried out? What intervals? What documentation? Relevant interested parties involved?						
f) Are periodic reviews and, if required, revisions to emergency preparedness and response procedures carried out?						
g) If required, are emergency preparedness and response procedures and plans reviewed and revised following periodic tests or emergency situations?						
h) Are actions from emergency response exercises carried out and followed up?						
i) Are results of emergency response exercises communicated to those who need to know about them?						
EMS (Environmental Management System) Emergency Preparedness and Response						
a) Has a procedure been established to identify and respond to potential emergency situations and potential accidents that can have an impact(s) on the environment?						
b) Is procedure implemented and maintained effectively?						

		O K	P P	O B	O F I	N C	N A
c)	Do we respond to actual emergency situations and accidents and prevent or mitigate associated adverse environmental impacts? Any examples?						
d)	Are periodic reviews and, if required, revisions to emergency preparedness and response procedures carried out?						
e)	If required, are emergency preparedness and response procedures and plans reviewed and revised following incidents or emergency situations?						
f)	Are periodic emergency tests of emergency preparedness and response procedures carried out? What intervals? What documentation?						

OBJECTIVE EVIDENCE / COMMENTS

Incident Investigation	O K	P P	O B	O F I	N C	N A
SMS (SAFETY MANAGEMENT SYSTEM) Incident Investigation a) Has a procedure been established to record, investigate, and analyze incidents? Does it define the requirements for b), c), d), and e) below? b) Are the underlying OHS deficiencies and other factors that might be causing or contributing to the occurrence of incidents determined? c) Is the need for corrective action identified? d) Are opportunities for preventive action identified? e) Are results of investigations communicated? f) Are investigations performed in a timely manner? g) Are required corrective actions or opportunities for preventive action carried out? h) Are the results of incident investigation documented and maintained?						

OBJECTIVE EVIDENCE / COMMENTS

Sources referenced in the development of this sample integrated management system audit checklist:

- www.scribd.com/doc/1035015/OHSAS-18001-2007
- www.isopocketguides.com/media/docs/QSCheck.doc
- www.scribd.com/doc/2563663/iso-9001-2000-why
- www.scribd.com/doc/2910021/ISO-9001-BY-KASHIF
- www.tlcnh.com/download/ISO14001ChecklistSample.pdf

Appendix B

This is a PowerPoint presentation on Performance-Based Safety: Modern Measurements for Modern Times. It can be used to help provide evidence of the issues needing attention as part of your efforts to consider the maturity of your safety management system as part of your overall integrated management system.

Performance-Based Safety©
Modern Measurements for Modern Times
CSHEMA 2006
Anaheim, California
July 15-20, 2006

Safety Measurement Rationale

" If You Don't Know Where You Are Going, Chances Are You Will End Up Somewhere Else" Yogi Berra

If you're not keeping score, it's just practice

Ronald D. Snee - Tunnell Consulting

Why Measure?

- Without adequate and appropriate measures, it's <u>virtually impossible</u> to <u>(intentionally)</u> improve 'any' business process, including safety performance.

- <u>Plus - Measuring badly</u> can be worse than not measuring at all.

Establishing Performance Measures

Each organization must create and communicate performance measures that reflect its unique strategy.

Dr. Robert S. Kaplin, Harvard Business School

There is no one right way to do it. Each organization must determine its own "right way".

Dan Petersen:Techniques of Safety Management, 3rd Edition, ASSE,

History of Performance Indicators for OHS

Typical Measures

Conventional : Lost time injury rates, Frequency and Severity rates, Fatalities, first aid cases, etc.

("reactive" or "lagging" indicators sometimes referred to as 'safety statistics')

Modern: Performance to standards or benchmarks, proactive measures of health and safety (ie: number of audits, scores of audits, behavioral observations, goals and targets achieved against those set, perception survey results

Sometimes know as leading indicators

Leading Indicators (Upstream)

Leading indicators are the performance drivers that communicate <u>how</u> outcome measures are to be achieved.

Robert S. Kaplan and
David P. Norton,
The Balanced Scorecard

Why Leading Indicators?

- Although leading indicators are sometimes more difficult to define and measure, they provide vital input to leaders in an organisation

- WHY - to assure them that complacency is being avoided and that continuous improvement is being sought.

- In very safety conscious organisations, a mixture of proactive and reactive indicators will be measured and trends followed with keen, but not impracticable targets, set to drive improvement.

The Safety Scorecard
Using Multiple Measures to Judge Safety System Effectiveness
Occupational Hazards - 05/01/2001

- 1. The effectiveness of safety programs cannot be measured by the more traditional factors in successful programs (injury rates, etc.)

- 2. Better measures of safety program effectiveness is the response from the entire organization to questions about the quality of the *safety management systems*, which have an effect on human behavior relating to safety.

- "I cannot stress enough the importance of having a clearly identified H&S program against which goals can be established at all levels of the organization, and people held accountable for before-the-fact measures of injury and illness prevention."

(Gene Earnest, former safety director for Proctor&Gamble USA)

The Challenge

- Proactive measures are <u>more difficult to set and measure</u>.

- However -organisations usually develop greater maturity in measuring performance as a result of such measures becoming progressively more of a focus.

Consider: Variables that consistently relate to lower injury rates
(Institute for work & health 2002)

- Monitoring at risk behavior and worker/work practices
- Having continuous and regular safety training
- Employee health screening
- Regular evaluation of occupational hazards
- Good housekeeping, safety maintenance and controls on machinery and equipment

Does your safety management system characterize these variables?

Better still, how do you <u>measure</u> them?

And even <u>better still</u>, if you measure, how do you evaluate their *effectiveness?*

How did we get here?

Who do we have to convince to get where we want to go?

- Measurement of OH&S requires assessment of the <u>process</u> involved in the management system, rather than measurement of outcomes (such as incident and accident rates)
- "Management of outcome instead of improvement of the system is destructive and is considered tampering" (Motzko, 1989)
- See – safety incentives

Basic Safety Performance Improvement Steps

- 1. Undertake a strategic planning session(s) to determine what you want to measure, why, and how that information will be used
- 2. Structure and develop your performance measurement plan. . . what will you track and how will you track it?
- 3. Establish measures, targets or other performance benchmarks or standards
- 4. Measure, evaluate, react and provide feedback
- Determine improvements or recognition opportunities, if desired

How do you measure safety?

Don't just count injuries and illnesses

Kyle B. Dotson ISHN 04/30/2001

- Focus on the effectiveness of the upstream processes put in place to control risk

- There's power in measuring the process rather than just the results, ie. (defects, injuries)

- This means measuring the effectiveness of management systems put in place to identify, assess, control, and continuously improve the risk profile of an organization

The Scorecard Approach

The trend today is toward multiple measures to assess safety system effectiveness

These usually include at least a balance of 5 measures:

- 1. The accident record
- 2. The audit
- 3. Perception survey results
- 4. Goals set compared to goals reached
- 5. Behavioral findings (safe vs. unsafe work related behaviors

The Challenge

"If you always do what you've always done, you'll always get what you've always got"

If you don't know where you're going, any road will take you there

Other references:
*http://siri.uvm.edu/ppt/perfmeas/
*http://www.c2e2.org/news_items/performlist.htm
*http://www.safetyxchange.org/article.php?id=244&cha_id=4

Appendix C

This is a PowerPoint presentation that you can use to help profile the features and benefits of an integrated management system. It can be used to profile those aspects of an integrated management system that an organization should consider in developing its strategic approach to an IMS.

What is a Management System?

A management system is the framework of policies, processes and procedures used to ensure that an organization can fulfill all tasks required to achieve its objectives. It encompasses all areas of operations.

What is a Quality Management System?

- Defined policies and procedures that provide a formal framework describing the way an organization conducts its core business.

- Defines all organizational processes and their interaction.

- The performance of each quality management procedure generates objective evidence by which to measure the performance of the organization and its management.

- PLAN – DO – CHECK – ACT cycle to manage by fact, ensure consistency, process control and continuous improvement.

- Common elements with other systems (HSE, Environmental, etc.) System through which information collected in all systems is strategically analyzed.

Evolvement of Quality

Quality Control: Focused on fulfilling quality requirements. QC involves the measurement of a product or service against a specified criteria to determine if it is acceptable or not.

Quality Assurance: Focused on providing confidence that requirements will be fulfilled. Sufficient checks and balances are built into the service provision or manufacturing process to ensure only good products or services are produced.

Quality Management: Coordinated activities to direct and control an organization with regard to Quality. Establishes sufficient controls to ensure that all organizational processes contribute to the provision of products and services that will satisfy the customer. Quality Management pushes the organization towards continual improvement.

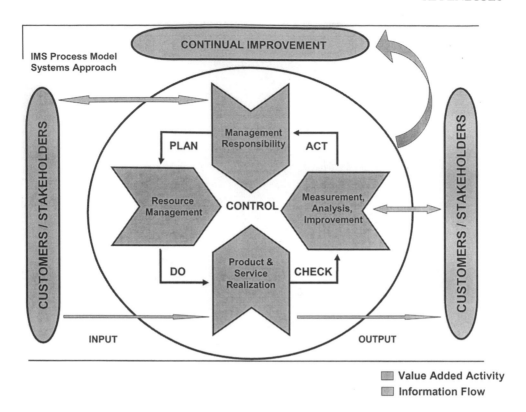

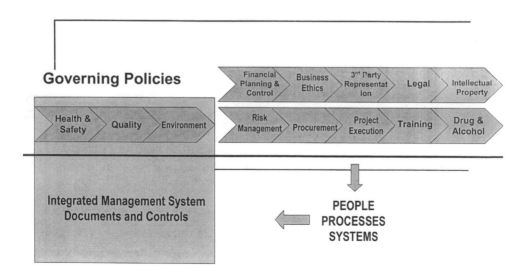

INTEGRATED MANAGEMENT SYSTEM

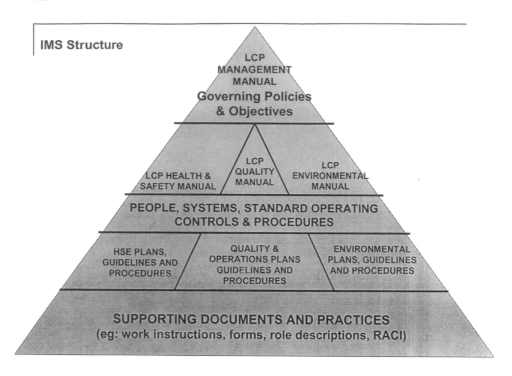

IMS Structure

LCP MANAGEMENT MANUAL
Governing Policies & Objectives

LCP HEALTH & SAFETY MANUAL | LCP QUALITY MANUAL | LCP ENVIRONMENTAL MANUAL

PEOPLE, SYSTEMS, STANDARD OPERATING CONTROLS & PROCEDURES

HSE PLANS, GUIDELINES AND PROCEDURES | QUALITY & OPERATIONS PLANS GUIDELINES AND PROCEDURES | ENVIRONMENTAL PLANS, GUIDELINES AND PROCEDURES

SUPPORTING DOCUMENTS AND PRACTICES
(eg: work instructions, forms, role descriptions, RACI)

IMS Systems Model   **Commonalities & Synergies**

Health & Safety CSA Z1000

PEOPLE PROCESSESS SYSTEMS

Quality ISO 9001

PEOPLE PROCESSESS SYSTEMS

Environment ISO 14001

Management Responsibility

Leadership, Involvement of People, Policy & Objectives, Customer Focus, Planning, Responsibility & Authority, Communication, Management Review

Resources & Systems Controls

Human Resources, Competency & Training, Infrastructure & Equipment, Working Environment, Manuals & Guidelines, Procedures, Document & Data Control, Records

IMS Systems Model   **Unique Processes**

PEOPLE
PROCESSESS
SYSTEMS

PEOPLE
PROCESSESS
SYSTEMS

Product & Service Realization

Planning, Legal &
Regulatory
Compliance,
Controls,
Implementation,
Emergency
Prevention,
Preparedness &
Response,
Management of
Change
Monitoring &
Measuring

Planning, Regulatory
Compliance, Design,
Contracts Mgmt.,
Procurement,
Production & Service
Provision,
Management of
Change Calibration,
Monitoring &
Measuring

Planning, Legal &
Regulatory
Compliance,
Environmental
Aspects & Impacts,
Controls, Emergency
Prevention,
Preparedness &
Response, Checking,
Evaluation of
Compliance

IMS Systems Model   **Commonalities & Synergies**

PEOPLE
PROCESSESS
SYSTEMS

PEOPLE
PROCESSESS
SYSTEMS

Measurement, Analysis & Improvement

Monitoring & Measurement, Nonconformance (Incident, Accident, Near
Miss) Control, Analysis of Data, Internal Audits & Assessments,
Corrective Action, Preventive Action, Lessons Learned, Communication

Appendix D

This is a PowerPoint presentation on the use of technology in your integrated management system. It is designed to support the chapter on technology uses for your integrated management system.

Using Technology in Safety To Work Smarter, Not Harder
31st Annual CSSE Professional Development Conference
November 18-20, 2001, Vancouver, BC
Wayne Pardy, Quality Plus Inc.

If you don't know where you're going, any road will take you there"

Alice In Wonderland

KPMG survey on Business Ethics
Globe & Mail, February 21, 1997
Top 10 issues of "ethical risk"

- **Integrity of records**
- **Worker Health & Safety**
- **Security of Internal Communications**
- **Quality and Safety of Products and Services**
- Receiving bribes
- Discrimination
- Sexual Harassment
- **Reporting Fraud or Compliance Failures**

Paradigm Shift

- Improving the quality of the industrial safety movement will depend on innovative people who are willing to shed the blinds of tradition- **William Pope - Safety Excellence: The Changing Emphasis**
- "The domain of risk analysis and safety is too often characterized by soaring and obfuscating rhetoric supported only by snake oil analysis" - **W. Kip Viscusi. Duke University**
- Motherhood rhetoric will always be the path of choice for those who can't or refuse to justify and rationalize safety initiatives based on sound reason and measured judgement- **Wayne Pardy, COH: 1995**

How Society is changing (or has already changed!)

- Shifting/changing demographics: values of society
- Employment trends: move to *information/knowledge based industries*
- Massive restructuring, reengineering, downsizing, layoffs, etc.
- Who is your "customer" for your "safety product"?
- "What" is your safety product?
- Are your safety initiatives relevant anymore (says who?)

The Future of Work

Sponsored by the Speakers Forum, Spring 1997

- **Technological innovation - Future work will depend more on <u>what we know</u> than on what we do...workers need specialized and broad based skills**
- **Information technology means that people no longer have to work in an office - mobility of technology applications**

- **Safety is basically an "information rich" area. . . The key is translating all that "information" into meaningful knowledge**

The End of Work

Jeremy Rifkin

- More than 14,000 workers die from accidents in the U.S. each year
- 2.2 million suffer disabling injuries
- ILO cites "job stress" as the biggest causal factor, yet most investigation forms don't acknowledge it, most compensation agencies don't compensate for it, and most management choose not to validate it...therefore, it doesn't exist!
- NIOHS study says that clerical workers who use computers suffer inordinately high levels of stress
- Most legislation is aimed at "rules & rule breaking" - WHY?

What do we want safety technologies to achieve?

- "Assessing" you current system of workplace measurement
- Identifying the key areas of "measurement"
- "Measuring" workplace perceptions toward <u>safety</u>
- Determining the appropriate "performance indicators" for your safety system
- Effectively and efficiently gathering the "data" needed to drive continuous improvement
- Enable us to react, and make corrections <u>quickly</u>

Pardy & Associates Safety Technology Survey- 1999
"Rate the Effectiveness of Your Safety System"

- Safety Audits - 33%
- Behavior-Based Safety Observations - 21%
- Injury Frequency and Severity Rates - 92%
- Accident and Property/Equipment damage costs - 18%
- Perception Surveys - 14%
- Bench Marking with other companies - 11%
- % Safety Goals Achieved (Strategic Planning) - 21%
- Total Workers' Compensation Costs - 76%
- Inter-Industry/Competitive Industry Rankings - 66%
- Medical Aid or Disabling Injuries - 91%
- Management Systems - 19%

Positive Performance Indicators for OHS
National Occupational Health & Safety Commission
Commonwealth of Australia

Typical Measures

Traditional: Lost time injury, Frequency rate, & % budget to remedy hazard

Transitional: Trend analysis and savings achieved through prevention

Modern: Performance to standards or benchmarks, positive measures of health and safety (ie: number of audits conducted and scores of audits conducted, perception surveys, "safe"-VS-"at risk" observations)

BHP Minerals Benchmarking Study
1995
"Best In Class Characteristics"

- A strong management commitment, reflected by a clear corporate policy statement, and the application of a consistent safety system. The use of select experts at the managerial level to strategically target safety improvement initiatives
- A close relationship between staff safety professionals and senior management
- Requirement of 'quality' safety performance as a condition of employment for managers, supervisors and employees
- Including safety in performance evaluations for managers, supervisors and employees
- Clearly defining lines of responsibility with respect to safety
- Establishing safety goals and targets
- Conducting safety audits
    - **"How does/can Technology fit into this picture?"**

Variable which consistently relate to lower injury rates

- Health & safety training of OH&S Committee members
- A participatory management style and culture that includes:
1. Empowerment of workers in key decision areas
2. Autonomy and control over work
3. Encouraging the long term commitment of the workforce
4. Good working relationship between management and workers
- An organizational philosophy on OH&S which includes
1. Delegation of safety activities to workers
2. Active participation of top management
3. Regular safety audits

- Monitoring at risk behavior and worker/work practices
- Having continuous and regular safety training
- Employee health screening
- Regular evaluation of occupational hazards
- Good housekeeping, safety maintenance and controls on machinery

Does your safety system exhibit these characterize these variables?

If so, how do you evaluate their *effectiveness?*

Caution. . . Injury Statistics Don't Tell The Whole Story
COS, July/August, 1999 - The Pardy Line

- Measurement Examples:
- *Systematic inspections of the workplace using a standardized checklist approach, checking the conditions against established standards*
- *Safety tours and observations of the workplace, work practices, or physical conditions*
- *Audits or other similar assessments of your safety system*
- *Observation techniques of conditions or practices (can include various equipment standards or personal practices or compliance to work methods, rules or standards)*
- *Degree of risk management improvement - "quantify"*
- *Safety improvement targets - have they been met/reached/achieved*
- *# of safety improvement suggestions made by staff*

Why safety performance measurement?

- Accurately measure effectiveness of achieving objectives
- Used to assist in business planning and performance improvement exercises
- Provides opportunity to "re-calibrate" prevention initiatives
- Provides opportunity for feedback
- Can be preemptive or predictive

What is a Safety Management System?

A comprehensive, integrated system for managing safety which sets out

- ## Specific safety objectives
- ## Systems and procedures by which these are to be achieved
- ## Performance standards which are to be met
- ## The means by which adherence to these standards is to be maintained

Regular monitoring/measurement with technology can include

- Obtaining information on relevant aspects of safety performance to check that objectives and performance criteria are being met
- Monitoring the use of procedures and checking of safety systems and equipment
- Identifying non compliance with the requirements of the safety management system, investigating them and taking appropriate corrective action
- Maintaining a system of records which demonstrates compliance with the safety management system

How did we get here?

Where we want to go with our safety technology?

- Measurement of the performance of the OH&S management system consequently requires assessment of the process involved in the management system, rather than measurement of outcomes (such as incident and accident rates)
- "Management of outcome instead of improvement of the system is destructive and is considered tampering" (Motzko, 1989)
- Process safety management approaches to OH&S performance measurement rely on continual monitoring of indicators of performance of the relevant processes, and continuous improvements in these processes

Basic Performance Improvement Steps - using a technology solution

- 1. Undertake a strategic planning session(s) to determine what you want to measure, why, and how that information will be used
- 2. Structure and develop your performance measurement plan. . . what will you track and how will you track it?
- 3. Establish measures, targets or other performance benchmarks or standards
- 4. Measure, evaluate, react, feedback
- Determine improvements or recognition opportunities

Q5AIMS Performance Assessment Technology
Objectives of the system:

To enable the safety system to be more accurately managed through a PC based source

To "add value" to existing paperwork, and can actually eliminate the need for paper work

To assign and track measures of the quantity and quality of safety management initiatives

To ensure timely and appropriate follow up on select safety activities

To measure the effectiveness of internal safety standards

To provide a safety reporting system not dependant on accident or injury statistics

To assist in the development of safety action plans

To ensure responsibility and accountability for safety management is assigned

To Identify opportunities for improvement

To facilitate legislative compliance and document due diligence efforts and processes

The Top 6 Challenges of Safety Technology Management

- Measuring organizational and employee results
- Using competencies in a performance management system
- Performance management tools to improve organizational effectiveness
- Supporting/evaluating your current safety culture Linking reward systems to performance management
- Developing and implementing safety performance management standards
- Aligning people with goals and corporate strategy

Appendix E

This is a PowerPoint presentation on the Characteristics of a Modern Health and Safety Management System. It can be used to help profile the aspects of a safety management system that should be aligned with other aspects of your integrated management system.

Characteristics of A Modern
Health & Safety Management System

- A **system** is defined by identifying all interrelated processes and their interdependencies

- A **system** is managed as a system of interrelated processes

- A **system** is improved by continuous measuring and evaluating all related processes

---

How do Accidents happen?
(Relative to the IRS model for Health & Safety)

- **Management structure** (duties & responsibilities under OH&S Act)
- **Management actions, priorities and behavior** (current safety culture)
- **Supervisory behavior** (OH&S expectations)
- **Tactical errors- workers** (OH&S expectations)
- **Accident/Incident**
- **Injury/Damage**

Leadership

- Corporate Policy Statement for OH&S
- Organizational Standards for Health & Safety Performance
- Corporate Manual OH&S Policies
- Safety Standards Manual
- Establishing Action Plans and Targets
- Authority & Responsibility
- Active Management & Worker Participation

Risk Management

- Risk Groupings
- Accident/Incident Analysis
- Job Planning
- Work Practices and Procedures
- Standard Protection Code
- Legislative Compliance

Education & Training

- Supervisory & Management Development
- Employee Training
- OH&S Committee Training
- OH&S Meetings
- General Promotion
- OH&S Communications
- Public Safety

Protection & Control

- Personal Protective Equipment
- Maintenance & Inspection
- Occupational Health
- Emergency Preparedness
- Fire Protection

Monitoring

- Worksite/Practice/Equipment Inspections
- Investigations
- Safety System Audits
- Industrial Hygiene Assessments

Culture

- Safety should be an integral aspect of all operations
- Management commitment, active participation and leadership
- Employee commitment to mirror senior management commitment

What is A Corporate Safety Culture?

- A Safety culture consists of a number of shared beliefs, practices, attitudes and behaviors.
- It is the atmosphere created which shapes the actions of the people who work in the business in question
- What are the characteristics of your culture

Factors for a <u>Successful</u> Safety Culture

- Top Management Commitment and Active Participation
- Policies and Procedures
- Action Plans and Targets
- Middle Management Involvement
- Supervisory Performance
- Employee Participation and "Buy-In"
- Flexibility
- Perception of a Positive Safety Culture

Accountability

- Safety action plans and targets are established (specific & reasonable)
- Safety activities and performance is actively measured
- Costs are identified and accountabilities assigned
- Performance expectations are defined
- Shared responsibilities are **clearly** defined

Modern Safety Management
Corporate Safety Strategy
"Statement of Principles"

Underlying philosophy of any Canadian safety system will be consistent with that of the IRS (Internal Responsibility System)

Direct & Contributive Responsibility
What is it?
How can it work on a practical, day-to-day basis?

Direct responsibility & Contributive responsibility for OH&S (as part of the Canadian legislative approach to the Internal Responsibility System for OH&S)

- ## Direct responsibility for safe production:
  extends to those who are directly responsible for the organization of work, the design of work practices and the manner in which, and the conditions under which, work is performed. . . Direct responsibility falls to worker, supervisor, management and executive

1981- Burkett Commission

Contributive responsibility

- Contributive responsibility extends to those who, although not directly responsible for the performance of work, are in a position to contribute to safe production through consultation, advice, audit or inspection

- <u>Contributive responsibility falls to health & safety committees, safety departments, unions, government</u>

Corporate Performance Standards
"How we are going to get there"

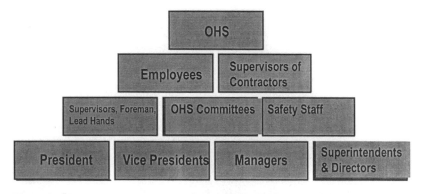

Everybody has to "share" in the responsibility for achieving successful safety performance. . . What can we <u>individually</u> and <u>collectively</u> do to ensure your safety performance is as good as it can be?

Where does your Internal Responsibility System need to go?

- From dependence – safety person responsible for all safety issues, including safety statistics, inspections, enforcement, etc.
- To independence – management and workers taking responsibility for their own health and safety
- To inter-dependence – management, workers, committees, safety professionals, sharing in the success and strategy of effective prevention initiatives

NOTES

Chapter 1

1. International Organization for Standardization, *Guidelines for the Justification and Development of Management System Standards*, 1st ed., ISO Guide 72:2001(E) (2001), 16.

2. Ibid.

3. Ibid.

4. Larry Martof, "Management Review: A Process, Not an Event," www.modernsteel .com/Uploads/Issues/October_2006/30758_quality.pdf.

5. www.qualitydigest.com/june05/articles/02_article.shtml.

Chapter 2

1. International Organization for Standardization, *Guidelines for the Justification and Development of Management System Standards*, 1st ed., ISO Guide 72:2001(E) (2001), 16.

2. Ibid.

3. Ibid.

4. Ibid.

5. Ibid.

6. Ibid.

7. Ibid.

8. Ibid.

9. Ibid.

Chapter 3

1. Royal Society of Chemistry, Environment, Health and Safety Committee note on Occupational Health and Safety Management Systems, version 1, June 12, 2005, pages 4–5.

2. www.scribd.com/doc/1035015/OHSAS-18001-2007.

221

3. *ILO Guidelines on Occupational Safety and Health Management Systems* (Geneva: International Labour Office, ILO-OSH, 2001).

4. Ibid.

5. The complete original text of the nonmandatory guidelines is found in the *Federal Register* 54 (18): 3094–3916, January 26, 1989. When OSHA announced a proposed rule in its 1990s regulatory agenda, the agency articulated its intent to have a mandatory standard that would include at least the following elements: management leadership of the program; active employee participation in the program; analysis of the work site to identify serious safety and health hazards of all types; training; and program evaluation. All of these components are present in the ANSI Z10 standard.

6. Specific national consensus standards (e.g., American National Standards [ANSI]), which the Secretary of Labor adopted on May 29, 1971, were either used as a source standard and published in Part 1910 as an OSHA standard or explicitly incorporated by reference in an OSHA standard.

7. Bryce E. Carson Sr., president and CEO and STR Registrar LLC (STR-R). www.str-r.com.

8. "Reproduced with the permission of Canadian Standards Association from CAN/CSA-Z1000-06, Occupational Health and Safety Management, which is copyrighted by CSA, 5060 Spectrum Way, Mississauga, ON L4W 5N6 Canada. While use of this material has been authorized, CSA shall not be responsible for the manner in which the information is presented, nor for any interpretations thereof. For more information on CSA or to purchase standards, please visit our website at www.shopcsa.ca or call 1-800-463-6727."

9. SafetyXChange, www.safetyxchange.org.

10. Canadian Standards Association.

11. Ibid.

12. National Safety Council website, www.nsc.org/resources/dod-matrix.aspx. Special thanks to Carol Brink-Meissner, program analyst with the Office of the Deputy Inspector General for Policy and Oversight, Department of Defense Office of Inspector General. The authors are grateful to Carol for her help and suggestions in highlighting the relevance of this comparative analysis during the course of their research for this book. This comparative analysis was performed in support of the evaluation of the Department of Defense Safety Program. Additional information on the mission of the Department of Defense Inspector General is available at www.dodig.mil.

13. Canadian Standards Association.

Chapter 4

1. Thomas R. Krause, John H. Hidley, and Stanley J. Hodson, *The Behavior-based Safety Process: Managing Involvement for an Injury-free Culture* (New York: Van Nostrand Reinhold, 1990).

2. Ibid.

3. Wayne G. Pardy, *Safety Incentives: The Pros and Cons of Award and Recognition Programs* (Orange Park, FL: Moran and Associates, 1999).

4. Ibid.

5. Ibid.

6. Ibid.

7. Ibid.

Chapter 5

1. James M. Ham, commissioner, *Report of the Royal Commission on the Health and Safety of Workers in Mines* (Ontario, Toronto, Canada: Ministry of the Attorney General, 1976).

2. Ibid.

3. James M. Ham, commissioner, *Report of the Royal Commission on the Health and Safety of Workers in Mines* (Ontario, Toronto, Canada: Ministry of the Attorney General, 1976), 5.

4. Ibid.

5. Ibid.

6. Tom Smith, Mocol, Inc., 2465 Eaton Gate, Lake Orion, MI 48360, www.mocalinc.com. Reproduced with the express permission of Tom Smith. Tom Smith of Mocal, Inc., is a leading North American consultant on management consulting to improve quality, productivity, and safety. When Tom first wrote this article for *Professional Safety* in February 1996, he was laying the groundwork for the business realities that the introduction of the twenty-first century would bring. As Tom's challenge is as valid today as it was in his original 1996 article, the authors felt it would only be fitting to let the reader get another look at what we feel to be one of the seminal articles written on the safety/quality relationship.

Chapter 6

1. E. Scott Geller, "Behavior-based Safety: A Solution to Injury Prevention: Behavior-based Safety 'Empowers' Employees and Addresses the Dynamics of Injury Prevention," *Risk & Insurance* 15, no. 12 (October 1, 2004): 66.

2. Thomas R. Krause, John H. Hidley, and Stanley J. Hodson, *The Behavior-based Safety Process: Managing Involvement for an Injury-free Culture* (New York: Van Nostrand Reinhold, 1990): 25–27.

3. Ibid., 56–57.

4. www.behavioral-safety.com/images/White.pdf, 5.

5. Ali M. Al-Hemoud and May M. Al-Asfoor, "A Behavior-based Safety Approach at a Kuwait Research Institution," *Journal of Safety Research* 37, no. 2 (2006): 2001–6.

6. Ibid., 6–8.

7. William C. Pope, "Operational Mishaps and the Involvement of Management," National Safety Management Society (1989), www.nsms.us/pages/opermishaps.html.

8. Petersen cited in Jose Perezgonzalez, *Construction Safety Management—A Systems Approach*, Dublin (2005).

9. E. S. Geller, *The Psychology of Safety: How to Improve Behaviors and Attitudes on the Job* (Radnor, PA: Chilton Book Company, 1996): 36–39.

10. www.ascc.gov.au/ascc/AboutUs/Publications/ArchivedDocuments/HealthSafety ResearchReport/2HealthandSafetyManagementSystems.htm#2.4.2.

11. Donald J. Eckenfelder, "Behavior-based Safety: A Model Poisoned by the Past; Based on Obsolete Thinking, Behavior-based Safety Isolates Safety Instead of Integrating It," *Risk & Insurance* 15, no. 12 (2004): 65.

12. Ibid.

13. Stephen H. Reynolds, "The Importance of Learning the ABC's of Behavioral Safety," *Professional Safety* (February 1997): 23–25.

14. Morton Hunt, *The Story of Psychology* (New York: Anchor Books, 2007), 275.

15. Alfie Kohn, *Punished by Rewards* (Boston: Houghton Mifflin, 2001): 42–43.

16. Frederick Herzberg, "One More Time: How Do You Motivate Employees?" *Harvard Business Review* (January-February 1968).

17. Ferdinand F. Fournies, *Coaching for Improved Work Performance* (New York: Van Nostrand Reinhold Co., 1978): 44.

18. James P. Womak and Daniel Jones, *Lean Thinking* (New York: Simon and Schuster, 1996): 48.

19. Peter R. Scholtes, *The Leader's Handbook* (New York: McGraw-Hill, 1998): 82–85.

Chapter 7

1. W. E. Deming, *Out of the Crisis* (Cambridge: MIT Press, 1986): 23–24.

2. Thomas A. Smith, "A New Loss Control Management Theory," *Accident Prevention* (July/August/September 1988): 5–10.

3. International Organization for Standardization, "Understand the Basics," www.iso .org/iso/iso_catalogue/management_standards/understand_the_basics.htm.

Chapter 8

1. "Your Plain Language Guide to C-45, OHS and Due Diligence," *Safety Compliance Insider* 2, no. 8 (August 2006): 14–15.

2. Ibid.

3. Ibid.

4. Ibid.

5. Ibid.

Chapter 9

1. www.intelex.com.
2. www.q5systems.com.
3. www.Steton.com.
4. www.csstars.com.
5. www.aonsafetylogic.com.
6. www.etq.com.
7. www.harrington-group.com.
8. www.syntexsolutions.com.
9. www.amadeussolutions.com.

SELECTED BIBLIOGRAPHY

Al-Hemoud, Ali M., and May M. Al-Asfoor
"A Behavior-Based Safety Approach at a Kuwait Research Institution." *Journal of Safety Research* 37, no. 2 (2006): 2001–6.

Brink-Meissner, Carol
Program analyst with the Office of the Deputy Inspector General for Policy and Oversight, Department of Defense Office of Inspector General.

Canadian Standards Association
CAN/CSA-Z1000-06. Occupational Health and Safety Management, 5060 Spectrum Way, Mississauga, ON L4W 5N6 Canada.

Carson, Bryce E., Sr.
President and CEO and STR Registrar LLC (STR-R). www.str-r.com.

Cooper, D.
"Behavioral Safety Approaches: Which Are the Most Effective?" (2007). www.behavioral-safety.com/images/White.pdf.

Deming, W. F.
Out of the Crisis. Boston: MIT Press, 1986.

Eckenfelder, Donald J.
"Behavior-based Safety: A Model Poisoned by the Past; Based on Obsolete Thinking, Behavior-based Safety Isolates Safety Instead of Integrating It." *Risk & Insurance* 15, no. 12 (2004): 65.

Fournies, Ferdinand F.
Coaching for Improved Work Performance. New York: Van Nostrand Reinhold Co., 1978.

Geller, E. Scott.
"Behavior-based Safety: A Solution to Injury Prevention: Behavior-based Safety 'Empowers' Employees and Addresses the Dynamics of Injury Prevention." *Risk & Insurance* (October 12, 2001): 66.

The Psychology of Safety: How to Improve Behaviors and Attitudes on the Job. Radnor, PA: Chilton Book Company, 1996.

Glendon, A. Ian, Sharon Clarke, and Eugene F. McKenna
Human Safety and Risk Management. Manchester, UK: UMIST, April 24, 2006.

Ham, James M.
Commissioner, *Report of the Royal Commission on the Health and Safety of Workers in Mines.* Province of Ontario, Toronto, Canada: Ministry of the Attorney General, 1976.

Herzberg, Frederick
"One More Time: How Do You Motivate Employees?" *Harvard Business Review* (January 1, 2003).

Hunt, Morton
The Story of Psychology. New York: Anchor Books, 2007.

International Labour Office
ILO Guidelines on Occupational Safety and Health Management Systems. ILO-OSH 2001. Geneva: International Labour Office, 2001.

International Organization for Standardization
Guidelines for the Justification and Development of Management System Standards. *ISO Guide* 72: 2001(E). 1st ed. Geneva: International Organization for Standardization, 2001. *Understand the Basics.* www.iso.org/iso/iso_catalogue/management_standards/understand_the_basics.htm.

Kohn, Alfie
Punished by Rewards. Boston: Houghton Mifflin, 2001.

Krause, Thomas R., John H. Hidley, and Stanley J. Hodson
The Behavior-based Safety Process: Managing Involvement for an Injury-free Culture. New York: Van Nostrand Reinhold, 1990.

Martof, L.
Management Review: A Process, Not an Event. (2006). www.modernsteel.com/Uploads/Issues/October_2006/30758_quality.pdf.

National Safety Council
"The Comparative Analysis Model: Mapping and Analyzing Safety and Health Management Systems." www.nsc.org/resources/dod-matrix.aspx.

NCS International
Comparison of AS/NZS4801:2001 with OHSAS 18001:2007. (2007). www.ncsi.com.au/downloads/OHSAS18001requirementsversusAS4801Rev1.pdf.

Pardy, Wayne G.
Safety Incentives: The Pros and Cons of Award and Recognition Programs. Orange Park, FL: Moran and Associates, 1999.

Perezgonzalez, Jose
Construction Safety Management—A Systems Approach. Dublin (2005).

Pope, William C.
"Operational Mishaps and the Involvement of Management." National Safety Management Society (1989). www.nsms.us/pages/opermishaps.html.

Reynolds, Stephen H.
"The Importance of Learning the ABC's of Behavioral Safety." *Professional Safety* (February 1997): 23–25.

Royal Society of Chemistry, Environment, Health and Safety Committee
"Note on Occupational Health and Safety Management Systems." (June 12, 2005): 4–5.

Safety Compliance Insider.com.
"Your Plain Language Guide to C-45, OHS and Due Diligence." Volume 2, no. 8 (August 2006): 14–15.

Scholtes, Peter R.
The Leader's Handbook. New York: McGraw Hill, 1998.

Smith, Thomas A.
"A New Loss Control Management Theory." *Accident Prevention* (July/August/September, 1988): 5–10.

Smith, Tom
Mocol, Inc., 2465 Eaton Gate, Lake Orion, MI 48360. www.mocalinc.com.

Womak, James P., and Daniel Jones
Lean Thinking. New York: Simon and Schuster, 1996.

Web-Based Resources and References

Government of Australia
Health and Safety Research Report on Health and Safety Management Systems. www.ascc.gov.au.

OHSAS 18001 blog.
ohsas18001expert.com/.

Pardy, Wayne G.
"CSA Z-1000: The New Canadian Standard for OHS Management." SafetyXChange: The Online Community for Safety Pros (June 6, 2006). www.safetyxchange.org.

Munro, R. A., and W. J. Luka
"OSHAS 18001 Puts Safety First." *Quality Digest*. www.qualitydigest.com/june05/articles/02_article.shtml.

SELECTED BIBLIOGRAPHY

Scribd.com.
    www.scribd.com/doc/1035015/OHSAS-18001-2007.
    www.scribd.com/doc/2563663/iso-9001-2000-why-.
    www.scribd.com/doc/2910021/ISO-9001-BY-KASHIF.
    www.scribd.com/doc/1035015/OHSAS-18001-2007.

Total Logical Concepts.com
    www.tlcnh.com/download/ISO14001ChecklistSample.pdf.

ABOUT THE AUTHORS

Wayne Pardy has been a practitioner in the safety and quality management fields for the past twenty-five years. Author of the book *Safety Incentives: The Pros and Cons of Award and Recognition Programs*, he has written extensively on safety and quality management issues in numerous Canadian and American publications, including *OHS Canada* magazine, *Canadian Occupational Health & Safety*, *Industrial Safety and Hygiene News*, *Compliance* magazine, *Accident Prevention* magazine and *Occupational Health and Safety*. He has been a frequent speaker at national conferences and professional development seminars in Canada and the United States. He is a past winner of the CSSE President's Award for his two-part series on "Building an Effective Safety System: Key Strategies for Maximizing Resources and Minimizing Losses," and his feature article on "Worker Empowerment and Joint Health and Safety Committees" won the Chilton Editorial Award. As a member of the Board of Advisors of SafetyXChange, which includes some of the continent's most respected thinkers, industry leaders, and policy-makers, Pardy has been a regular contributor to SafetyXChange for their economics of safety series.

As an original founder of Q5 Systems Limited, and most recently their vice president of QHSE Management Services, Pardy has assisted many national and international companies in establishing and improving their management systems through the use of leading-edge web-based and mobile technologies for audits, inspections, and action tracking. During his time with Q5 he was an associate member of the technical advisory committee of the Canadian Standards Association in the development of the Canadian OHS management system standard, Z1000:2006.

Currently a quality management consultant with Quality Plus, Inc., he is currently the chair of the Minister's Advisory Committee on Occupational Health and Safety for the province of Newfoundland and Labrador, Canada.

Terri Andrews is a systems consultant with a focus on the development, implementation, improvement, and assessment of QHSE management systems within a diverse range of industries. She has helped numerous organizations achieve registration or recognition of their management systems to various standards and requirements, including ISO 9001:2000 (quality), ISO 14001:2004 (environmental), ISO 17025 (laboratory practices), CSA Z1000 and OHSAS 18001 (health and safety), ANSI/ASC Z1.13 (quality for basic and applied research), CWB, NVLAP, NQI Canadian Quality Criteria for Public Sector Excellence, and various medical and governmental regulatory approvals (FDA, GMP, etc.).

For almost twenty years, Terri has guided dozens of organizations through the design, management, and improvement of operational and management policies, procedures, and documentation across all organizational functions, including strategic and upper management, human resources, procurement, design, construction and fabrication, service delivery, production, QHSE system management, and quality improvement (corrective action, incident management, lessons-learned systems, auditing, etc.). Her work has spanned a wide range of private and public sectors, including oil and gas, manufacturing, research and design, service, aviation, education, government, tourism, aquaculture, and medical and laboratory facilities.

Ms. Andrews regularly develops and delivers a varied range of QHSE seminars and training sessions, including internal auditor courses, risk analysis, and HSEQ tools. As a certified lead auditor in both ISO 9001:2000 and ISO 14001:2004, she conducts registration audits on behalf of QMI and third-party assessments for her clients. She is a senior member of ASQ and was one of the founders of ASQ in the province of Newfoundland and Labrador.